D1008650

From Training to
Performance Improvement

Jim Fuller
Jeanne Farrington

From Training to Performance Improvement

Navigating the Transition

Jossey-Bass
Pfeiffer

San Francisco

Copyright © 1999 by the International Society for Performance Improvement (ISPI)

ISBN: 0-7879-1120-8

Library of Congress Cataloging-in-Publication Data

Fuller, Jim.
   From training to performance improvement : navigating the transition / Jim Fuller, Jeanne Farrington.
      p.   cm.
   "Sponsored by International Society for Performance Improvement (ISPI)."
   Includes bibliographical references and index.

   ISBN 0-7879-1120-8 (acid-free paper)
   1. Employees—Training of. 2. Employee motivation. 3. Labor productivity. I. Farrington, Jeanne. II. International Society for Performance Improvement. III. Title.
   HF5549.5.T7   1999
   658.3'14—dc21   98-40231

Printed in the United States of America

Published by

350 Sansome Street, 5th Floor
San Francisco, California 94104-1342
(415) 433-1740; Fax (415) 433-0499
(800) 274-4434; Fax (800) 569-0443

Visit our website at: www.pfeiffer.com

Acquiring Editor: Larry Alexander
Director of Development: Kathleen Dolan Davies
Developmental Editor: Susan Rachmeler
Editor: Philip Holthaus
Senior Production Editor: Dawn Kilgore
Manufacturing Supervisor: Becky Carreño
Cover Design: Laurie Anderson

Printing   10   9   8   7   6   5   4   3   2   1

Contents

Figures and Exhibits

Figures

Exhibits

Foreword

This book will enable you to explore the benefits of human performance technology (HPT) and to manage the transition from training to performance improvement. Use the ideas in this book to help you convince your clients and your organization about the business benefits of going beyond training and adopting the human performance approach. The authors, Jim Fuller and Jeanne Farrington, have had many years of practical and successful experience making the case for HPT and managing the process of moving a variety of organizations from training to performance improvement. They share their most successful processes in a very persuasive, systematic, and effective way in this book.

In my view, one of the primary benefits of this book is that it attempts to eliminate an ironic and negative situation facing corporate training specialists. Most thoughtful trainers have realized in the past few years that training is a solution to knowledge problems. Although many business goals require new knowledge, experienced trainers understand that achieving business goals also requires other kinds of performance enhancements in addition to training, for example, motivational or organizational change. One of my consultant friends calls training one of the key "corporate aspirins." In the past, training has too often served as a placebo or "sugar pill" for business problems. When training is aimed and fired at problems caused by motivational issues or organizational glitches, the investment is wasted. Because we seldom perform cost-benefit analyses of training, we have allowed ourselves to think that training might have had an impact. Yet there has been a gradual realization that training alone is not working as expected.

Many experienced trainers and managers know that achieving their business goals often requires organizational change and/or motivational enhancement rather than training. Because it has become evident over time that most training is expensive and yet does not fully achieve business goals, the support for training has diminished in many corporations. The emphasis in the past few years has been on "minimalist," "on-the-job," and "action learning" approaches that greatly reduce the investment in training design and delivery. Training and trainers are "at risk" in this environment.

Training specialists who have used the broader and more effective human performance approach report surprisingly positive results. The human performance improvements and associated financial gains have been exciting. Many feel that at last we have an approach that will allow trainers to be viewed as direct contributors to business successes. As a result, many changes are occurring in the profession. Consider these developments:

> The two largest international professional associations of trainers, the International Society for Performance Improvement and the American Society of Training and Development, have decided enthusiastically to go beyond a narrow focus on training and adopt the human performance model for the foreseeable future.

> Many universities are no longer educating corporate training specialists. Many of them have either already switched their undergraduate and graduate programs to an emphasis on performance improvement, or they are in the process of making the change.

A number of key management consulting groups have adopted the HPT model in their work and report very positive reactions from their clients.

The experience of training professionals who have had the opportunity to use this model in business settings is universally positive.

Yet these developments are wrapped into an ironic advancement. Only a few of the largest business organizations and very few midsize organizations are aware of the benefits of the HPT approach for their business strategy. Early corporate adopters of the HPT approach tend to be organizations undergoing rapid change and a constant challenge to find new ways to grow—for example, the larger high-technology, banking, communication, and service industries. Managers in these industries who have expanded the role of training to add motivational and environmental strategies for increasing performance have concrete evidence of its financial and human benefits.

Thus we are faced with a major gap between the approach adopted by nearly an entire professional field, on the one hand, and the speed of adoption of the HPT approach by most organizations, on the other. This gap is an extraordinary opportunity for trainers. The authors describe ways to close that gap and take advantage of the benefits. They provide wonderful examples, details, arguments, case studies, and processes for helping organizations make this essential transition. Jim and Jeanne have drawn on their own experience, as well as the experience of other professionals who have "been there," to write a clear and practical guide about how to make an effective transition. As authors they share very positive but unusual qualities. Their combined experience in this field totals about thirty-five years. They both have successfully managed large-scale human performance initiatives in business settings. They are both excellent and popular instructors in our University of Southern California's human performance technology master's and doctoral programs. I've been honored to work with them and learn from them. I hope that you will have the same pleasure and benefit from their book that I have experienced.

February 1999   Richard E. Clark
                                   Professor of Educational
                                       Psychology and Technology
                                   Director, Doctoral Program in
                                       Human Performance Technology
                                   University of Southern California

Preface

In 1992 the *Handbook of Human Performance Technology* (Stolovitch and Keeps, 1992) was published. It was an immediate success among performance improvement professionals who were seeking information on the growing field of human performance technology (HPT). Since reading the handbook, many professionals have struggled to implement HPT within their own organizations. The need for specific information and recommendations regarding how to implement HPT within organizations has grown rapidly. Unfortunately, there have been few resources to really assist with the transition to HPT. It has been unclear how a training department can navigate this uncharted journey to become a performance improvement department.

The purpose of this book is simple. We want to provide you with a road map for your HPT journey. We have already been down the HPT road and we made the trip successfully. We have learned about the pitfalls, potholes, and potential wrong turns firsthand. We have discovered that the fastest route isn't always the shortest route to success. We'd like to share our experience with you so that you can have a safe and enjoyable trip.

Like *Managing Performance Improvement Projects* (Fuller, 1997), this book is written in a rather casual and conversational style. *From Training to Performance Improvement* is not an academic dissertation about the theoretical underpinnings of HPT. We discuss foundational issues only when necessary to understanding why we are recommending a specific course of action. We have designed the book as a practical guidebook to help you navigate the transition to HPT. We have included models, specific implementation plans, and plans to prepare for the journey. This is a book about doing. The success of the book will be measured by your success in navigating the transition to HPT.

Now let's take a look at what lies ahead.

Chapter One examines the need to make the transition from a training focus to a performance focus. We look at why organizations train and why training often does not achieve desired results. To help in understanding the transition from training to development, we present two case studies in which an organization begins to see the need for the performance technology approach.

Chapter Two explains HPT. We begin with the theoretical basis and cover the process for analyzing performance improvement problems. To ensure that you don't get into early trouble, we cover some common pitfalls that you will want to avoid.

In Chapter Three we address the issue of human capital. You need managerial support and sponsorship to transition effectively from training to performance. Human capital is a hot management topic, and HPT provides powerful tools for increasing the value of human capital in your organization.

Making the transition to HPT requires planning and careful implementation. Chapter Four shows you how to prepare for implementation to ensure a successful start.

Once the preparations are complete, you are ready to start implementing HPT in your organization. Chapter Five explains how to select and manage your first performance improvement projects successfully.

For an organization to take an HPT approach, there must be some awareness that HPT exists and that it is available to be used. Chapter Six lays out strategies for increasing the organization's awareness for HPT. Will you be ready to put out the sign that reads "Performance Technology Department"?

The transition from training to performance improvement is not a smooth journey. You will experience some implementation problems. Chapter Seven identifies the common barriers to adoption and implementation and helps you plan how to get around them.

Do you want to change your entire training department into a performance improvement department? It's not an easy task. In Chapter Eight we address the process for making the transition.

Experienced performance improvement professionals are hard to find. There is a serious shortage in the labor market. Thus you'll probably need to develop performance consultants from within your organization. In Chapter Nine we examine the knowledge and skills that qualified performance consultants need and explain how you can help them to develop that knowledge and those skills.

Chapter Ten looks at the roles and responsibilities of the manager of HPT. If this is your career goal, you'll want to start planning now. The position is as demanding as it is strategic.

Before you begin your journey, you might want to check where you are right now. We have both met numerous people at conferences who hand us business cards indicating that they are performance consultants, human performance technologists, or performance technologists. But when we ask them what they do, it turns out that they are still in the training business. Because of HPT's current popularity, many training departments have tried to jump on the HPT bandwagon simply by renaming themselves the "performance consulting group" or something similar. Clearly this is a case of a sheep in wolf's clothing.

To be clear on where you are starting, here is a location check. Look back at the major performance improvement interventions that you or your department have implemented during the past year. Sort each performance improvement project into one of these three categories:

1. Training and job aids were the only solutions implemented.

2. Training and nontraining solutions were used to improve performance.

3. Only nontraining solutions were necessary to improve the performance.

If you have a real performance improvement department, you'll find that your projects are close to evenly spread across the three categories. You'll also know that you have arrived at your destination when you have clear and compelling measures of the bottom-line impact of your performance improvement projects.

Now, with your feet planted firmly where you really are, let's begin the journey.

February 1999   Jim Fuller
San Jose, California   Jeanne Farrington

For Jim's grandmother,
Olga Woods
and Jeanne's mom,
Hazel L. Dolph

Acknowledgments

Many people contributed, whether they knew it or not, to writing this book. There are the people we learned from, clients who presented interesting problems, folks who voiced dissenting opinions, and friends and family members who enriched our spirits. We do not have the space to list everyone who has helped us, so please forgive us if we left out your name.

For their professional or academic influence on one or both of us, we acknowledge with gratitude, Dick Clark, David Cox, Mark Eisley, Tom Gilbert, Joe Harless, Erica Keeps, Johanna Keirns, Al Lowe, David Migocki, John Morlan, Harry O'Neill, Don Perrin, Allison Rossett, Jim Russell, Darryl Sink, and Harold Stolovitch. For their support and encouragement in a variety of important ways, we want to thank Larry Alexander, Kathleen Dalton, Fred Estes, Rob Harris, Jyoti, Patrick and Merra Lee Moffitt, Russell Park, and Cindy Vinson.

We appreciate the efforts of our families, as well, and all the supportive contributions they made. Many heartfelt thanks go to Shawn Brenneman and Jim Sr., Lois, Bob, Josh, and Sarah Fuller.

From Training to
Performance Improvement

1

Discovering Human Performance Technology

T he futurists predicted the end of paper in the office. New technology would create the paperless office where all documents were in electronic format, logically stored for rapid recall, and always up-to-date. The reality has been a bit different. If you work in today's office, you'll see more paper than ever. The futurists were wrong. Very wrong.

The futurists also predicted a decreasing need for employees within organizations. They predicted that new technologies would decrease the need for office personnel as well as for people to execute processes to create products. They were wrong again. Unemployment is driving toward an all-time low; indeed, there is a painful shortage of available labor. The transformation of industry has created the role of the knowledge worker and such workers are in short supply. The leading business experts are saying that people are the last remaining competitive advantage (Pfeiffer, 1994). In an effort to create a competitive workforce, organizations are investing heavily in their human capital.

Training to Develop Human Capital

Organizations are spending billions of dollars every year to train their employees. They must be expecting something back in return. Why do organizations send their employees to training? A group of

1

highly respected, well-known managers offered the following inter-esting insights:

> "I send people to training because I want them to be able to perform better. I need them to increase their ability to do their jobs. We just need a better training department, because our training doesn't seem to be achieving results."

> "Confidentially, I'd like to do away with training inside the organization. I have yet to see a single training program pay off. It's a huge expense that I would do away with if I thought that I could get away with it."

> "Well, I guess we send folks to training because we don't know what else to do. If they're not performing, it's got to be because they don't have the skills. Right?"

> "We have a long history in investing in our employees. I think it's really a symbol that we think people are important. It shows that we care."

> "Don't get me started. Training is a big dark rat hole that we keep pumping money into. It's become an entitlement pro-gram that we can't possibly kill. If we have to cut expenses, it's the first place I go."

The perspectives of these managers raise some serious issues. Managers want to improve the performance of their own employ-ees and the organization as a whole. They are sending their employ-ees to training to achieve this improved performance, but they don't believe that the training is actually achieving its goal.

Questioning Training's Role

When Jim's son was six years old, he got into Jim's tools and selected a pipe wrench for himself. It was big, heavy, and red. It offered everything a young boy could want in a tool. He spent the remain-der of the afternoon using his newfound tool. He pounded nails with it. He drove screws with it. He even used it to "saw" (actually "split") some small boards in two. Jim was less than impressed with the results that his son created with the pipe wrench. There was nothing wrong with the pipe wrench. It was designed to tighten and loosen pipes, which it does quite well. It simply makes a poor hammer, screwdriver, or saw. The problem was misuse of the tool; Jim's son was asking it to do things that it wasn't made to do.

Many organizations are suffering from the same problem. They are asking training to do too much. Training is designed to increase the skills and knowledge of people; if it is well designed, training can accomplish this end very well. We get into trouble when we expect training to accomplish other things. Training is a poor tool to change employee motivation or employee attitudes. It's also a poor substitute for a clear job description or for being provided with the right equipment to perform the work one is assigned.

Why are organizations asking training to accomplish more than it's capable of doing? There are several reasons. First, most organizations have a training department, which naturally has a vested interest in providing training. The training manager is in the business of selling the importance of training to the organization and then providing it when asked to do so. Second, employees ask for training. They may have several different motives for wanting to go to training. Third, it is very difficult to establish whether training is or isn't meeting its objectives. Fourth, and finally, many managers are unfamiliar with other performance improvement alternatives. The managers of various functions are too busy managing their end of the business (for example, R&D or sales) to find out about alternatives. It's easier to delegate the problem to the training manager, who is happy to take the business. Training is an easy answer. But what's the question?

Training May Not Always Work

Very few people would say, "I have a pesticide problem." The real problem is insects in the house. Pesticide is one potential solution, and installing screens to keep the bugs out of the house in the first place is another. "I have a water problem" is rarely heard. "Fire" is the real problem. Water is a solution to the fire problem. But if it's a chemical fire or an electrical fire, water will actually make the problem worse. Both of these statements are rather silly, and represent backward thinking. They demonstrate a solution in search of a problem. "I have a training problem" is another example of backward thinking (Mager, 1992). Unless you are doing training poorly, you don't have a training problem. Performance is the real problem. Training is a potential solution, but not always the correct or sufficient one to resolve the performance problem.

The Call for a Different Approach

If training isn't always the answer, what is? How will we know when training *is* the right answer? What we need is a different approach. Rather than being focused on providing training, the organization needs to be focused on improving performance.

The shift from a focus on training to a focus on performance improvement is a significant transition for an organization. Both the employees and the managers are in the habit of asking for training, not for better performance. There is a training department that knows how to implement training, but where is the performance department? Who in the organization has experience solving performance problems? What process is used? What tools are available? An organization cannot simply decide that from now on they will be "performance-focused." They won't be. The transition is a significant organizational change that requires planning and effort to be successful.

The Difference Between a Training Focus and a Performance Focus

So how will you know when your organization is focused on performance? Performance improvement is focused on improving the organization's ability to achieve its objectives. It looks at outcomes that are valued by the organization, typically measured in cost, quality, quantity, or timeliness. One of the early indications that you have begun the transition will be a shift in your objectives. Let's look at a few examples to get a clearer picture.

Following are some objectives from the sales department of an organization. Read all three and identify the one that is focused on performance improvement.

1. Sales reps will understand the need to manage their sales funnel.
2. Given a list of prospects, the sales reps can identify high potential sales.
3. Sales reps will meet their quotas with consistent and stable sales results.

Let's check your answer. If you look at answer 1, it's rather obvious that this objective does not demonstrate a focus on performance. Just because the sales reps understand a need does not mean that they will actually do anything to address that need, or if they do, that they will achieve any increased results. Answer 2 describes a pretty good training objective, but it's not a performance focus. Identifying good prospects is a skill that the sales reps may need, but it does not ensure increased sales. Answer 3 is focused on performance. The organization and the sales reps both value high and consistent sales. This is the reason the organization has sales reps. A performance improvement effort would be focused on answer 3.

Ready for another example? This time let's look at some management objectives and try to determine which one is focused on performance.

1. Managers will know how to manage budgets.
2. Managers will create budgets for their organization.
3. Managers will achieve their business objectives while remaining under budgetary limits.

Answer 1 is not focused on performance. What it describes is not even a good training objective. Answer 2 is focused on behavior, not on performance. A manager can create a budget and still spend inappropriately. Behaviors do not necessarily result in performance. The performance-based answer is 3. The organization wants managers to achieve results while managing finances according to the budget.

Here is our last example. Which of the following manufacturing objectives is focused on performance?

1. Maintenance personnel know all the machinery on the manufacturing floor.

2. Maintenance personnel perform specified maintenance on all machines.

3. Machine downtime is less than four hours per month.

Again, answer 1 is not even a good training objective. What does it mean to "know" the machinery? Answer 2 is another statement designed to drive behavior, not performance. It is actually possible to perform scheduled maintenance and have downtime increase. The real performance-focused statement is answer 3. It states a specific outcome that is valued by the organization, one that has an impact on cost, quality, and quantity.

Case Studies: Discovering HPT One Step at a Time

The focus on performance was not invented by somebody who just woke up one morning and decided everything needed to change. The transition was born out of failure. Organizations created training programs to accomplish specific business goals. Many of them failed. As they examined why, they began to see the need for a different approach, one focused on performance. Tools and methods started to be developed to aid in improving performance. The new approach needed a name, so the term *human performance technology* (HPT) was born. People who use HPT are referred to as human performance technologists, performance technologists, or performance consultants.

The shift to HPT is best understood by examining examples. We can learn a lot from the successes and failures of others. Here are two case stories that capture one organization's journey from training to performance technology.

The Problem Isn't Always Obvious

One large technology company was not immune to the pervasive "training problem" approach. Its training department created training courses for many different skill areas. Employees took them, lots of them. But in the midst of this burgeoning training activity, something caught management's attention: an undeniable failure.

The company was in the business of creating software products. To increase the productivity of its software developers, management introduced a program called Software Reuse. Software Reuse is based on the realization that many software programs share common functions and therefore can share segments of code. Thus, rather than writing new code for every line of code for every software product, a software developer can create a software product by assembling blocks of code that have already been written. The company believed that its Software Reuse project could reduce development time by up to 80 percent. This obviously represented a significant competitive advantage for the company, and so a major initiative was launched.

Management asked the training department to create a training course on Software Reuse. Using sound instructional design practices and principles, the training department developed a Software Reuse course. The course ran for ten days and covered all the aspects of using Software Reuse techniques. As a capstone and final demonstration of readiness, the trainers had the class develop blocks of code, then put them together to create a simple product in class. The course went very well and was highly praised by course participants. The management team, the trainers, and the software developers all felt that they were adequately prepared to implement Software Reuse. However, performance back on the job was another matter.

Graduates from the Software Reuse class went to work on a major project, but they did not use any of the Software Reuse training they had received. Puzzled by this lack of implementation, the trainers concluded that the students had not adequately learned the materials. So they created a three-day refresher course and brought the training graduates back for some additional training. After completing the course, the software developers went back to their work environment and continued to do things "the old way," that is, they did not employ Software Reuse practices.

Frustrated with these results, the training group concluded that the source of the problem must be the students that had been selected as the pilot group for the training course. The trainers knew that their course was instructionally sound; thus the only apparent variable was the students. So the course was run a second time with a different group of students. But the results were the same: once they went back to work, none of the course participants used the Software Reuse approach. The training group was determined to discover the reasons why their training program was not producing the desired results back on the job.

After some investigation, the training team made a critical discovery: none of the software developers had access to the server where the code blocks were stored. The server the developers used lacked sufficient disk space to hold the library of code modules, so the library had been installed on the finance server. The financial controller was unwilling to give the software developers password access to the server that ran the payroll system (for some rather obvious and compelling reasons). Without access to the code building blocks, progress was halted. To solve the access barrier, the capacity of the software developer server was expanded and the library was installed on it. Software Reuse was in full swing for about a week, but then it stopped abruptly.

Determined to understand why the training was not succeeding, the training group continued their investigation. They discovered that the library of code modules had bugs. Lots of them. The software developers were spending more time fixing the modules than they would have spent writing the code from scratch. The R&D manager was a strong supporter of Software Reuse and championed an effort to fix the buggy code modules. Software developers were assigned modules to debug and place back into the library. After the bug problem was finally fixed, Software Reuse was used extensively for about a month, but then it was abandoned once again.

The training group was called in to determine what had gone wrong with the implementation of their training. The trainers were baffled. The software developers had demonstrated that they were able to implement Software Reuse in their day-to-day work environment. They obviously had the knowledge, skills, and resources necessary. A new barrier to performance must have developed. But what was it?

A week of investigation revealed no reasonable barrier to performance. Frustrated with their analysis, the trainers decided to convene a meeting of the Software Reuse graduates. The trainers closed the doors and told those assembled that anything they said inside the room would remain confidential but the training team really needed to know why the software developers had stopped using Software Reuse techniques. After much discussion the software developers finally revealed why they had stopped using the Software Reuse approach. The response shocked the trainers. The software developers felt that the management team didn't want them to implement Software Reuse, and that software developers who were implementing it were being punished.

The software developers had discovered that the management team had not changed the criteria for evaluating performance. Evaluations and pay increases were being driven by the old performance criteria: "amount of new code written." A software developer who

used the old method and wrote all new code took six months to produce a product. A software developer who used Software Reuse techniques would create only one-tenth the amount of new code and get
the product out in one month. Unfortunately, according to the performance criteria, the developer who used the old method would be
considered a top performer, while the Software Reuse developer
would be judged a bottom-level performer. The managers were using
a powerful reinforcer, pay, to reward old behaviors and punish new
ones. When confronted with this dilemma, the management team
immediately changed the performance criteria to reward Software
Reuse. Management met with all the software developers in the
organization and apologized for the confusion they had caused. The
new performance evaluation criteria were carefully presented and
explained. Before long, back at the job, developers who had not gone
through the training were spending time in the cubicles of those who
had, learning all they could about taking the Software Reuse
approach. Adoption of the practice spread like wildfire. The project
concluded well ahead of schedule and exceeded all sales projections.

The Software Reuse experience caused significant concern
throughout the training organization. It became clear that skills and
knowledge were important but were insufficient to achieve the
desired performance.

The Customer Isn't Always Right

After the Software Reuse experience, the training group realized
that they needed to take a new look at the skills and knowledge that
were needed to improve performance. When they received their
next training request, they decided to look beyond their traditional
training needs analysis.

The company's purchasing organization was requesting training in
the form of documentation. The purchasing department had implemented a new purchasing system that included a new computer program that was supposed to simplify the process of purchasing the
thousands of parts the company needed to manufacture its products.
The new system and its associated computer program were designed

to reduce both overstock and out-of-stock inventory situations while simultaneously maximizing the purchasing discounts the company received from its suppliers. After implementing the system, however, the company was experiencing just the opposite. Parts costs were going up, inventory was increasing, and out-of-stock situations were shutting down manufacturing several times each month. The purchasing management team had talked to the purchasers and concluded that training on the use of the new system was adequate but the purchasers were having problems with the new computer program. Therefore what was needed was better documentation that the purchasers could refer to when they could not remember how to use the software.

The management team's assessment seemed reasonable, but the training group decided to do some additional analysis. They wanted to ensure that the documentation would actually result in increased performance. Their interviews with personnel in the purchasing department revealed a consistent message: the purchasers all felt that they needed documentation in order to use the software. But during one of the interviews, one trainer happened to ask a purchaser if he used any other software in his job role. The purchaser beamed with pride as he listed word processing, spreadsheet, e-mail, and graphics packages that he knew how to use. Noticing no software documentation on the employee's bookshelf, the trainer asked why he could operate so many different software packages without documentation but not the purchasing software. When the purchaser became evasive, it became clear to the trainer that other issues were at play.

Additional investigation and work with the purchasing department revealed a startling issue. Within the purchasing organization there was a variable level of expertise in the purchasing process. When difficult purchasing issues arose, newer, less-experienced purchasers would ask a more capable member of the department to handle them. This informal system prevented errors from being made by aligning the expertise with the difficulty of the purchasing problem. But the new software system forced each employee to handle all aspects of his or her own accounts. A system that was designed to increase productivity was doing just that; unfortunately, the productivity it was increasing was error productivity. Thanks to the new system, less-experienced purchasers were able to make more mistakes in less time than ever before.

Why did the purchasers create a smoke screen by insisting on documentation? The purchasers had figured out that the new purchasing system could not be deployed until the documentation was in place. The process of creating documentation would take time and thus delay implementation of a system that none of the purchasers wanted. They preferred the old informal system that provided prestige to experienced workers and removed difficult tasks from novices. If the documentation were created, the purchasers would simply create a new reason that the system could not be implemented. Training was not the necessary solution. Robust change management efforts were what was needed to resolve this particular performance problem.

The training group would be forever changed as a result of the Software Reuse and the purchasing experiences. It was clear that training alone would not solve the performance problems they had encountered. In fact, they began to question whether they were in the right business. They were selling solutions (training) in search of a problem (improved performance). New thought systems and operating processes would need to be created to enable a shift from selling solutions to fixing performance problems.

Summary

In this chapter we have examined how training is used by organizations. Training is clearly not an all-purpose tool able to solve all performance problems. This calls for the transition to a different approach—human performance technology. HPT is focused on improving the performance of an organization as measured in terms of cost, quality, quantity, or timeliness. Its focus is not knowledge, skills, abilities, competencies, or behaviors. In the next two chapters we examine the major theory behind HPT and how to take a performance technology approach to improving performance.

2

Understanding Human
Performance Technology

Over the years we have met many individuals who have handed us business cards identifying themselves as performance consultants or human performance technologists. After hearing what they do as their daily work, however, we have realized that most of these self-described human performance technology (HPT) practitioners are really focused on training. They have a new vocabulary, and perhaps a new process chart, but they are still in the business of providing training.

The purpose of this chapter is to ensure that you have a consistent understanding of what HPT is before you begin planning how to do it. You may have several years of experience in the HPT field, or you may have done extensive reading in the area. We'd still like to encourage you to read this chapter. You may experience something new, or experience something familiar in a new way. In any case, reading this chapter will ensure that we are all on the same page before proceeding. Take the time to invest in developing a clear understanding of HPT.

Human Performance Technology: A Description

What is HPT? Many professionals have struggled to come up with a concise response. The HPT field is large, and it continues to grow. The *Handbook of Human Performance Technology* (Stolovitch and Keeps,

1992) does a good job of describing HPT and should be on the bookshelf of every HPT professional (that shelf of books you have actually read). To get us up and running, here is a quick, consistent definition:

> *Human performance technology* is a systemic and systematic approach to identifying the barriers that prevent people from achieving top performance that contributes to the success of an organization. We then create solutions that quickly and effectively remove those barriers so that people can improve their performance and achieve their full potential.

There is a lot of content to think about in that short statement. Let's begin by looking at the systemic element, then move on to the systematic elements.

People Perform Within a System

The Software Reuse experience discussed in Chapter One demonstrated that improving the knowledge, skills, and attitudes of employees was insufficient to improve their on-the-job performance. Performance is a much more complex issue. As we look at the barriers to performance, it becomes clear that people work within a performance system, with many external factors that affect their performance. Unless all the components of the system are operating correctly, it will be impossible to optimize performance.

Figure 2.1 illustrates the human performance system. It shows a system where organizational inputs, people, and their behaviors lead to performance, consequences, and feedback, which loops back through the system to the organization and the people in it, and so on. Moreover, the components of this system exist within an environment that also affects performance. Let's examine each component within the human performance system to understand how it affects performance.

Figure 2.1. The Human Performance System.

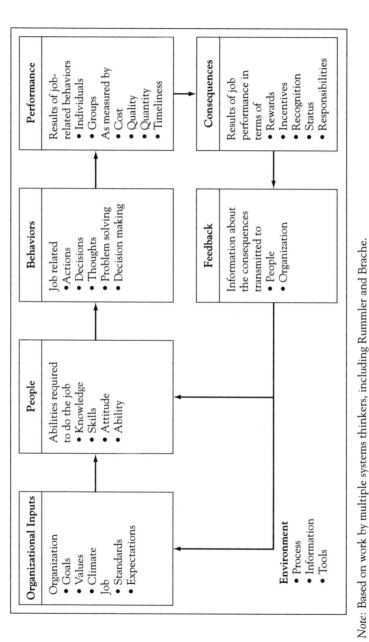

Note: Based on work by multiple systems thinkers, including Rummler and Brache.

Organizational Inputs

The system begins with organizational inputs (refer to the Organizational Inputs block in Figure 2.1). Every organization provides inputs to its employees or members. The inputs can be fixed or variable, formal or informal, documented or not documented, but they exist nonetheless. The organization also has goals, values, and an overall climate that affect the way people operate within it. Most organizations have a *culture*, or behavioral norm, that identifies how work is to be done within the organization and how members of the organization are to treat one another. Individuals who fail to adapt to the prevailing culture are socially punished by the group, choose to leave because they don't fit in, or are fired for failing to demonstrate teamwork (Aronson, 1995).

In addition, most organizations provide each employee with a written position plan that indicates what their role is within the organization and what results they are expected to achieve in their job. Ideally, this plan offers a clear picture; but if the position plan is poorly written or out-of-date (as often happens), the employee could easily end up striving to achieve the wrong performance objectives. We have seen instances of training programs where the most valuable outcome for the trainees was simply to gain a focused picture of management's job expectations. The employees knew how to do the tasks they were assigned, but they didn't know that management desired those specific tasks.

If there are performance barriers in this part of the process, employees are typically confused about their role in the organization. With poor inputs, they are forced to guess what the organization wants them to achieve. If they guess wrong, they are unpleasantly surprised when they receive poor evaluations (see the Feedback block in Figure 2.1) during their yearly performance evaluation (assuming that there is one) or during their job termination exit interview.

People

Inputs from the organization affect the people the organization employs (refer to the People block in Figure 2.1). People take the available input and use their existing knowledge, skills, and attitudes, resulting in various behaviors. If the capabilities of the people are inadequate, they may perform their tasks incorrectly, inadequately, or not at all. Like each component in the performance system, the capabilities of the people are a necessary but insufficient element in the process of achieving performance. The error typically made by most organizations is to focus exclusively on the people component of the human performance system and ignore the other components. This effort produces highly capable people who are struggling to produce results in a suboptimized environment. This creates high levels of frustration that have been demonstrated to increase attrition. High performers who can secure a position with another organization that has a less frustrating working environment will frequently do so (Greenberg, 1994).

Behaviors and Performance

On-the-job behaviors are influenced by organizational inputs and result in performance—the desired accomplishment for which the job exists. This performance can be at the individual or group level. Typically, performance is measured in terms of outcomes that are desired and valued by the organization, for example, reduced product costs, increased quality, or increased productivity. It is important to distinguish between behaviors and performance. Behaviors are measured in terms of specific actions or activities. Performance is measured in terms of outcomes. What makes the organization successful is performance, not behavior. Organizations that become obsessed with controlling or improving behaviors typically run into difficulty improving both individual and organizational performance (see our discussion of Performance Improvement Pitfalls at the end of this chapter). It is quite possible to have employees working within a system, demonstrating desired behaviors, and yet not achieving any desired outcomes.

Some organizations use a management philosophy commonly referred to as *management by objectives* (MBO). This method of managing sets clear performance goals (desired outcomes) and allows the employee to select the best method (within the guidelines of the organization's culture) to achieve the performance. The focus is not on employee behaviors but on their performance.

Consequences

Job performance has associated specific consequences (refer to the Consequences block in Figure 2.1). If the consequences reinforce the desired performance, then it is likely to continue. If the consequences punish the expected performance, then it is likely to extinguish over time. B. F. Skinner demonstrated this simple relationship in his experiments. When looking at causes for the performance problems of individuals or groups, we frequently find that incorrect consequences are the performance barrier. We have looked into organizations and found multiple examples of the following:

- Correct performance that was ignored (so why bother to do things right?)

- Correct performance that was punished (which discourages continuing with the performance)

- Incorrect performance that was ignored (so why improve or change?)

- Incorrect performance that was rewarded (which encourages continuing with the incorrect performance)

The consequences of performance should be aligned with the organizational inputs. When they are out of alignment, people are forced to choose between *what they are told to do* and *what actually gets rewarded* within the organization. When this occurs, most members of the organization are smart enough to give the appearance of following the organizational inputs, while spending most of their time doing what gets rewarded. This has long-term impact on the credibility of the management team within the organization. If management says to do "A" and rewards people for doing "B," employees rapidly learn to disregard what management tells them. (Wouldn't you?)

Feedback

Once the consequences are established, they need to be fed back to the people and the organization (refer to the Feedback block in Figure 2.1). A system that does not provide feedback is an open loop, one in which the results are likely to be unpredictable. When provided with regular feedback on their performance and the consequences of their performance, people will modify their own behavior to optimize their performance and the associated consequences. Without frequent, accurate feedback, people are far less likely to improve their performance over time.

Feedback needs to be coupled with performance. A young child who does something wrong in the morning and is punished that night after his parent returns from work is not going to associate the punishment with the earlier wrongdoing. It's much the same with performers in an organization. If the feedback on their performance is not given until a month later (say, during the department's regular update meeting) or (worse!) a year later (say, during a yearly performance review), the opportunity for reinforcing desired performance is greatly diminished, if not entirely lost.

We know of many cases where top performers left an organization because the organization failed to provide them with positive feedback regarding their contribution to the organization and how highly they were valued. Some discovered for the first time at their exit interviews that they were considered top performers who were being groomed for management positions.

Intelligent use of feedback alone can improve the performance of an entire organization. Take the case of a U.S. automobile manufacturing plant. The workers on the assembly line in this plant had never received any feedback concerning their own productivity as a team. Management kept careful records of the number of cars they produced but did not share that information with the workers. One evening, the night shift broke the record for number of cars produced on a single shift. Proud of this accomplishment, the night-shift manager wrote "Night Shift Breaks Record," followed by the number of cars produced, in large letters and numbers on the concrete floor of the assembly line. The night shift came to work the next night to find that the writing on the floor had changed. Now it read "Day Shift Breaks Record," with a production number one greater than the night shift had produced the night before. Not to be outdone, the night shift broke the day shift record by one car. This went back and forth for three months, with production increasing by one car per shift. This remarkable increase in productivity occurred because of one simple change: introducing feedback to the workers on how they were performing as a team.

Environment

The last component of the human performance system is the environment (refer to the lower left of Figure 2.1). Environmental factors include work processes, information, and tools, all of which can have a significant impact on performance. If people are given poor information and inadequate tools, how can they be expected to achieve optimal performance? Environmental flaws can seriously impede performance even if the organizational inputs, people abilities, behaviors, consequences, and feedback are of the highest quality.

The processes that people work within must enable top performance, not provide barriers to performance. Members of an organization who are "tied up in red tape" will not achieve breakthrough performance. If you put a great performer in a bad process, it is the process that will win, not the person. Imagine a situation in which people are trained in high-speed manufacturing practices, then placed in a manufacturing process where they have to wait around for parts to arrive. Sound silly? It happens.

Well-designed information sources are also a critical part of the environment. We worked with one organization that clearly demonstrated this issue. A group of workers was provided with terrible documentation on a complex process. The multiple steps (258 of them!) they were required to follow were hidden within four three-inch binders. Following the overly complex process required endless flipping through the binders or relying on memory. Not surprisingly, performance quality was unacceptable.

The best-trained people with the wrong tools won't achieve top performance either. Ever attempt to change a tire without a lug wrench? That doesn't sound like a formula for success, does it? One company was concerned about losing expensive replacement parts, so it limited the number of parts that their product repair people could check out and take to the customer site. If the engineer guessed right and brought exactly the right parts to repair the product (an infrequent occurrence), all went well. Usually, however, the engineer guessed wrong and then had to make multiple trips between the customer site and the office. This increased the cost of repair and angered the customer, who could not use the product until it was repaired.

Whole-System Solutions

If people are to achieve top-level performance, all the components of their human performance system must be optimized. With each barrier in the system, their performance decreases. As human performance consultants, our job is to remove as many of the barriers as possible or practical.

As Figure 2.1 illustrates, the human performance system has many parts. That is why training, all by itself, is an insufficient approach to improving performance. While training can have a positive impact on the people component of the human performance system, training cannot fix performance barriers in the areas of organizational inputs, consequences, feedback, or the environment. We need to create performance improvement solutions that can address each of the broken elements of the performance system.

The Causes of Top Performance

The concept of the human performance system was reinforced by a study conducted to determine *why* top performers excelled. The study examined top performers (defined as the top 15 percent) and median performers in the same jobs. Careful observation of performers' work led to identification of the causes for the performance differential. The results indicated several reasons for superior performance. As you read through the findings, refer back to Figure 2.1, with its schematic of the human performance system, and try to identify what part of the system was being optimized to improve performance. This exercise will not only help you to understand better the human performance system, it will also increase your insight into possible performance improvement solutions that you can use to deal with performance problems you may encounter.

• *Top performers do away with unnecessary steps.* Performers who are systems thinkers typically take a close look at the processes they use to achieve their objectives or results. If there are steps or actions in a process that are not really necessary to achieve the desired outcome, they eliminate those steps or actions from their work process. This could mean skipping steps 5 to 9 on the checklist or circumventing entire processes. This obviously allows these performers to achieve much more than other performers in the organization who are still doing unnecessary and time-consuming work.

• *Top performers implement an extra step that is needed but not documented.* Many times the documentation for a process or job responsibility leaves out several activities or actions that would speed up the process or ensure higher quality. Workers who keep notes on their failures and successes are quick to determine what additional steps or actions need to be taken to avoid failure or achieve success. They add these steps or actions to their regular work patterns until they become routine. Top performers who are responsible for the maintenance or repair of systems or processes are especially adept at finding these productive extra steps.

• *Top performers use available information and documentation that others do not.* Information in large organizations is frequently hidden or not well known. Some performers come across obscure information or documentation, such as diagrams, schematics, repair manuals, and such, that is not widely distributed throughout the organization. The information was available to anybody who knew where to look for it or who to ask for it, but most people didn't know. With this additional information in hand, the person can far outperform the other people in the organization who do not know about the information source.

- *Top performers develop their own self-created job aids that others lack.* Some top performers assemble or create their own job aids based on their work experience. Born from experience rather than theory, these job aids tend to be highly effective and give the owner a significant advantage over performers who have to discover the information for themselves each time they need it.

- *Top performers possess information/data that others don't.* The organization studied was quite large, with several sites that operated very independently. Different parts of the organization created information/data sources independently and typically did not inform the other parts of the organization that such "in-house" resources existed. Top performers were successful in scouting out sources of information outside of their own worksite that would assist them in their work. One stellar performer achieved his breakthrough performance based on information contained in a booklet generally available to every member of the organization but not generally known about.

- *Top performers possess better tools than others.* The organization described in the study made tools available to all performers, but some people ended up with better tools than others. In some cases the tools were software programs. In addition to the standard software on the system, the top performers looked for additional software tools from different sources. They then secured a copy for themselves and installed it on their system. In other cases, the tools were standard-issue equipment used for installing or repairing equipment. Top performers rapidly realized that the standard-issue tools were inadequate for the job and began to accumulate additional tools through other sources, usually at their own cost.

- *Top performers have a different motive for performing.* Different people possess different internal motivation factors. People who see their position as a temporary job bring different levels of energy and enthusiasm to their tasks compared with individuals who see their position as their life's work and passion. Some performers are promotion-minded and want to prove themselves. Others simply possess a stronger work ethic. This intrinsic motivation element can help performers take initiative in overcoming barriers in the performance system that the organization is not addressing.

- *Top performers receive different guidance and feedback.* Some managers and leaders within the organization possessed strong and highly practiced coaching skills. Others did not. Performers who worked for coaching managers received more frequent and better feedback on their performance. This allowed the members of their organization to examine their work practices and performance continually, leading to constantly improving performance over time.

- *Top performers receive different incentives.* Within a large organization there will be variability in management and leadership practices. Some managers understood the importance of recognition and reward. They also understood that what motivates one person may not motivate another. Top performers were found more frequently in organizations where managers understood basic motivation and how to use it effectively to achieve results within their organization.

- *Top performers do not excel because of training.* The issue of receiving more, different, or better training was not found to be a major contributor to top performance. The ability to optimize the other components of the human performance system appeared to be the key. As barriers were removed, performance increased dramatically.

Although training was not a significant contributor to the achievement of top performance, it was found to make major contributions to improving performance. The study also looked at the performance differentiators between the bottom 15 percent of performers and the median performers and found that for that group quality and quantity of training was the most significant issue. So, while training provided significant gains from poor to median performance, training did little to move median performers to being top performers.

The Performance Improvement Process

The human performance system explains how performance works within an organization. A wide range of variables affects the performance of people. Within a given system, one, many, or all the variables may be creating barriers to top-level performance. The barriers may affect all or some of the people in the system. How does a performance consultant determine what is broken within the system and how best to fix it?

As we mentioned earlier, HPT is systemic. We look at all the variables within the system to determine what impacts performance. But HPT is also systematic. We examine the human performance system using a process to ensure that we neither miss important factors nor jump to any conclusions. A large number of HPT models have been created over the years. They may differ in their appearance but most contain the essential elements of problem definition, root cause analysis, solution implementation, and evaluation. In this chapter we introduce the process that we designed for use at Redwood Mountain Consulting. Here we offer a brief overview. We discuss model selection and implementation more in depth in Chapter Four.

Phase 1: Problem Definition

The first phase of the HPT process is problem definition, where we determine what we are attempting to achieve. As Figure 2.2 shows, several activities occur in the problem-definition phase. A good performance improvement project always begins with the needs of the business. The purpose of performance improvement efforts is to affect performance that increases the organization's success. By starting and remaining focused on business needs, we keep our performance improvement efforts on course. While defining these business needs, we will want to define the desired outcomes of the project. How will we know when the project has met its goals?

Next we determine what performance is necessary from the people within the organization. We can compare the desired performance

Figure 2.2. The RMC Performance Technology Process.

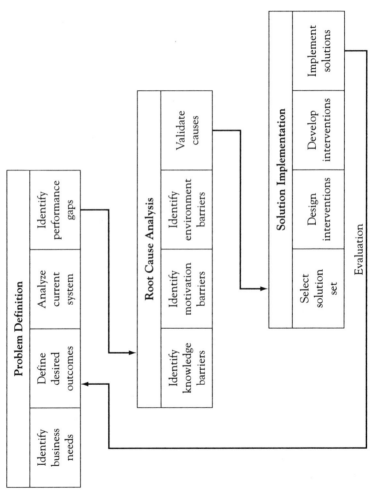

with the existing or current performance to identify what gaps actually exist. This prevents us from creating a performance improvement solution for performance areas that aren't broken.

Phase 2: Root Cause Analysis

Once we have identified the performance gap or gaps, we can proceed to the root cause analysis. Using root cause analysis tools borrowed from the quality movement, we can determine what is actually creating the performance gaps.

The list of validated root causes becomes the target for the development of the performance improvement solutions. If we can eliminate the root causes, we can achieve the desired performance, which leads to achieving the business need or goal. Solutions should be selected that specifically eliminate the identified root causes as efficiently and effectively as possible. The cost of eliminating the performance barriers should be weighed against the benefit of achieving the business need.

Phase 3: Solution Implementation

The implementation of solutions should be undertaken with attention toward implementation management (see Fuller, 1997) and change management issues. The effectiveness of the performance improvement project should be evaluated based on achieving the original business goals identified in the performance analysis phase.

We hope that this quick overview has given you a workable definition and a clear picture of human performance technology. The performance technology process is complex. This book offers only a brief overview of the process itself, for our main purpose is discussing management of the transition from a training process to a performance improvement process. Nevertheless, if you are serious about making this transition, you will need to know this process and methodology in depth. If you need more information on the process of HPT, we recommend the *Handbook of Human Performance Technology* (Stolovitch and Keeps, 1992). We also highly recommend that you attend local and national meetings of the International Society of Performance Improvement.

Next we need to cover some pitfalls that can ensnare the deployment of HPT within an organization.

Performance Improvement Pitfalls

Experience has taught us that there are several pits that you can fall into when it comes to improving the performance of people within organizations. Some are common misconceptions that cause us to focus on the wrong things, and others are stumbling blocks of our own choosing. Before continuing with the strategy for implementing systematic performance improvement, let's review a few of these pitfalls. As you read we invite you to ask yourself, "Is this a likely pitfall for me or my organization?" This will help you to be on the watch for such pits before you fall into one.

Overemphasis on Training

As human beings we tend to do things we know how to do well. We are creatures of habit and we find comfort in the known. Performance consultants who come from a training background need to be aware of this issue and be on guard against falling into old patterns. As training professionals we can easily see the knowledge gaps and the training solutions that would solve them. That approach is not systemic, however, and can leave significant performance barriers that suboptimize the results of the organization. This natural proclivity to look for training problems is made worse by the typical organization's tendency to ask for training to solve every performance problem it encounters. It's too easy to give the customers what they ask for.

Training is one of the many performance improvement solutions available to the performance technologist for improving the performance of individuals or organizations. Training may well be an appropriate solution for fixing a performance problem. As good performance consultants, we simply need to ensure that we do not overuse nor misuse training as a solution.

You may find that you or other performance improvement professionals fall into the training habit. It's easy to do. Indeed, it happened with some of Jim's early performance consulting staff at Hewlett-Packard. To break the habit, the staff adopted a specific strategy for about a year. First, we agreed that we would recommend training solutions only as a last recourse. Until we had examined all other methods for removing the performance barrier, we would not talk about training solutions. Second, we agreed that any performance consultant who was recommending a training solution had to convince his or her fellow performance consultants that it was the most effective and efficient method for eliminating the performance barrier. We found that this two-step strategy greatly improved our critical thinking in solution selection.

Competencies

Few topics have created more heated discussion among performance improvement professionals than competency modeling. Some believe that competency modeling represents the next great breakthrough in people development. Others believe that it results in very limited or no impact on business results. Regardless of your current position on competency modeling, let's take a look from an HPT perspective.

Competency modeling seeks to identify the competencies (or capabilities, if you prefer) that the organization needs to meet its business goals. These model competencies generally result in a people development plan that is focused on specifying behaviors or creating skills and knowledge throughout the organization. The most frequently selected solution for developing these competencies is training.

In terms of the human performance system (you might wish to refer to Figure 2.1), competency modeling is focused on the development of the people component of the system. Although it is an important component of the system, the people component is not the entire system. Like training, competency modeling does not address the entire performance system, and it leaves significant barriers to performance. We believe that it is better to take a more whole-system approach to improving performance.

The Cult of Behavior

In *Human Competence: Engineering Worthy Performance*, Tom Gilbert (1996) identifies an issue he calls the "cult of behavior." Gilbert identifies this issue as "the appeal to control or affect behavior in some way. There is little or no technology of ends and purposes. Indeed, behavior itself is viewed as an end rather than as a means to an end" (p. 7). As performance consultants, we need to be on guard to ensure that we do not fall into this pervasive trap. The cult of behavior typically manifests itself in one of three specific areas:

• *Work behavior.* This form of the cult values the expenditure of energy in the form of hard work, regardless of the results achieved by the work efforts. When caught in this trap, the tendency is to get everybody to work exactly like a specific top worker and to value activity rather than results. Once in an evaluation meeting a manager was praising the value of a certain employee. He told about the disasters this employee had fixed during the year. The other managers were about to demand this employee's immediate promotion, but then one manager asked, "Who started the disasters?" As it turned out, the employee who fixed all the disasters had been responsible for creating most of them in the first place.

• *Knowledge.* An organization in the grip of this form of the cult admires those who possess great stores of information, theory, and skills, regardless of whether the knowledge results in improved performance. When in this trap, the organization emphasizes people development. But placing highly developed people in a dysfunctional work environment does not necessarily result in improved performance.

- *Motivation*. An organization possessed by this form of the cult esteems eagerness and the display of positive attitudes. In this sub-cult, it doesn't matter what you achieve as long as you wear a smile, remain positive, and rally around the company objectives. When caught in this trap, the organization is typically focused on building morale and teamwork (not a bad thing, but usually insufficient by itself to improve performance). Some of the best and brightest engineers are cantankerous hermits. The person who dares to expose the faults in the plan may be the most valuable employee in the organization.

This overfocus on behaviors is particularly dangerous in the area of performance improvement. As performance consultants, our objective is to improve performance, not behaviors. The organization values (or should value) performance, not behavior. Specific behaviors do not necessarily lead to desired performance. Environmental or situational factors may prevent behaviors that worked for one person from working for another. Some employees will display all the right behaviors but never achieve the desired level of performance. Still others will display completely different behaviors and achieve superior performance. To illustrate the dangers of the cult of behavior, we offer the true story of Bubber.

Bubber was a sales representative for a large corporation, but more than a bit unusual for a man in that position. He did not look like a sales representative. Bubber was rather short and about seventy-five pounds overweight. He was the king of the $79 polyester business suit and typically wore a shirt that needed ironing, with a mismatched tie.

Bubber did not act much like a sales representative either. Bubber's company had set out very clear behavioral expectations for sales representatives. They were expected to spend very little time in the office and most of their time with customers (rather than knocking on customers' doors, Bubber spent his time at his desk at the sales office, talking on the phone, and either eating doughnuts or smoking a cigar). Sales reps were expected to put on conferences and invite new customers to them to hear about the company's products (Bubber never held these events). Bubber's sales district also had expectations regarding how many sales brochures were to be mailed to existing and prospective customers each month (Bubber never sent out mailings). New sales representatives were coached on how to dress to give the best impression and instill customer confidence (Bubber was obviously a nonexample).

Bubber's behavior was clearly outside the company's expectations. Why, then, wasn't he fired? Year after year Bubber consistently exceeded his sales quota, averaging 130 percent of quota. He always led the district, and frequently the region, in sales. He received numerous awards for his sales performance. The organization simply couldn't afford to lose an employee as valuable as Bubber. In the same sales district, new sales representatives who "dressed for success," mailed thousands of brochures, put on seminars, and were always out on the road visiting customers rarely did as well as Bubber. With few exceptions, they were all below quota.

Why was Bubber so successful? He was the king of networking. Bubber had long ago mastered "relationship selling." When Bubber was not at the office, he was attending every club and organization attended by businesspeople. Toastmasters, Lions, Rotary, Elk, Moose, you name it, he was involved. When he wasn't at fraternal meetings, he was golfing with businesspeople. Bubber knew everybody who did business in his sales district. When the company raised his sales quota, he simply "worked the phones," calling his customers and asking them to place extra orders. He'd also call businesspeople he'd just met and ask them to do him a favor by placing an order, "Just to try out the product and see if you like it."

Bubber's organization was mired in the cult of behavior. Its focus was on specific behaviors rather than on performance. Fortunately for Bubber, he was in a job where his performance had a specific, trackable, and clear measure: quota performance. Nobody could argue with his sales results. Had Bubber been in almost any other job in the company, he would have been let go long ago. With no clear and compelling performance measure to protect him, Bubber would have been judged on his behaviors and certainly found wanting.

Summary

In this chapter we have focused on mastering the basic HPT philosophy to prepare you for the following chapters on implementing HPT within your organization. Having a consistent understanding of HPT facilitates a smoother transition.

There are some main points to remember from this chapter:

- As performance consultants, we need to have a consistent definition of HPT.

- People perform within a system. When we affect the system, we affect performance.

- Barriers can exist anywhere and in any number within the performance system.

- Barriers left in the system suboptimize performance.

- HPT takes a systematic approach to identifying and removing performance barriers.

- HPT is driven by business needs and does not create solutions in search of a problem.

- The root causes of performance gaps must be identified and removed. We fix causes, not symptoms.

- As performance consultants, we do not overuse or misuse training as a performance improvement solution.

- We are aware of the "cult of behavior" and its ability to derail the implementation of HPT.

In the next chapter we look at why an organization would care about HPT. Knowing how to position and sell HPT is essential to ensuring a successful transition. Managers have a multitude of management techniques and processes available to them. Most managers have tried many new techniques, only to discover that they did not bring their promised results (Micklethwait and Wooldridge, 1996). Why should organization managers and leaders be interested in HPT? The answer lies in the shift to knowledge work and in the need to manage human capital better than ever before.

3

Driving the Value of Human Capital Within Your Organization

After reading the previous two chapters on the foundations of HPT, you may be wondering why this chapter is devoted to human capital. The answer is strategic and straightforward. To succeed in implementing HPT within your organization, you will need some high-level management support. Management provides funding for the organization, decides what strategies the organization will pursue, and most probably sets the charter for your organization.

Management and Human Capital

Historically, management has viewed training as the intervention of choice for improving the performance of employees. Training has many features that managers find attractive. First, it holds a great deal of face validity: it seems perfectly logical that if you want an employee to do a task better, he or she will need improved knowledge and skills to do so. Second, training as a performance solution has been reinforced throughout the manager's experience. The *Harvard Business Review* frequently features articles on training, but not much has shown up on HPT. Finally, training is very convenient. Organizations typically have an in-house training unit; thus the manager can delegate the identification and implementation of training solutions for the organization to the training unit.

The management team will require a compelling reason to begin thinking about systematic performance improvement. The best reason is the one that affects how they themselves are evaluated: business results. Human capital is an issue that is beginning to affect management teams in almost every organization. Today, management publications such as *Forbes*, *Fortune*, and *Business* frequently feature articles about the impending shortage of human capital, and about how managing human capital effectively will be the key to competitiveness in the future. The labor pool is drying up and many companies are experiencing serious difficulty finding quality workers, as the following examples illustrate:

- Bell Atlantic interviewed 57,000 people to find 2,100 sufficiently capable to be trained as operators and installers.

- Chemical Bank interviewed forty people to find one who could be trained as a teller.

- Pacific Bell tested 3,500 candidates for jobs that do *not* require a high school diploma; 95 percent of the candidates failed.

- Of the candidates applying for jobs at Motorola, 80 percent could not pass a seventh-grade English or a fifth-grade math test.

A Case Example of the Value of Human Capital

For the past twenty-five years, one company has stood out as the champion of the stock market. It posted the highest stock returns of any company from 1972 to 1998. This company's stock has split many times and has posted a total return of 34,477 percent, or 1:344. An investment of $2,900 made in 1972 would be worth $1 million today. This company's success is extraordinary. Others would like to duplicate its results. The mystery company's identity? Southwest Airlines.

To understand Southwest's success, you have to understand how it competes in an aggressive marketplace. Traditional sources of competition (Pfeffer, 1994) include the following:

Product technology: A company's product includes innovative technology that cannot be copied, and this technology gives the product an advantage in the marketplace.

Process technology: A company produces its product or provides its service in some manner that gives it a competitive advantage because of lower costs or a rival's inability to duplicate the product at all.

Protected and/or regulated markets: The company is a legal monopoly, protected by a city, county, state, or national agreement. The company faces no rivals and doesn't have to compete to sell its product or service. For example, the water company has a monopoly on supplying water to your home.

Special access to financial resources: Because a company has an established history of reliability, it can borrow money at a lower rate than its competitors, and thereby benefits from lower costs that can be passed on to the customer.

Economies of scale: The company can produce the product more inexpensively due to large volume, and then pass its lower costs on to the customer.

Unfortunately, these competitive advantages are quickly fading. New product technologies are rapidly copied. The secrets of process technology are revealed when competitors hire people away from their rivals. Today many utilities companies and other "protected" monopolies are being deregulated and losing their protected status. Venture capitalists will loan to anybody, and interest rates continue to be low. Smaller operations are producing their products at a lower cost than larger operations. Southwest doesn't gain a competitive advantage from any of these factors either.

Product technology: Southwest flies 737s and has no seat reservation system.

Process technology: Southwest sells a commodity product using standard, observable methods.

Protected and regulated markets: Southwest has actually had to overcome regulation; the company has never benefited from it.

Special access to financial resources: Southwest is the least leveraged airline in the United States (Southwest Airlines, 1998a).

Economies of scale: Southwest's 1997 $3.8 billion in revenue represents only a small portion of the air travel marketplace (Southwest Airlines, 1998b).

If it's not benefiting from any of the traditional sources of competitive advantage, how has Southwest Airlines managed to thrive in the cutthroat airline market? The company's competitive advantage is its highly motivated, productive, and performance-oriented workforce. Southwest succeeds because of its human capital. Thanks to its superior workforce, Southwest has won the "Triple Crown" award for airline service, meaning best on-time record, fewest lost bags, and fewest customer complaints. What's especially remarkable is that Southwest has won this award ten times, while no other U.S. airline has won it even once (Southwest Airlines, 1998b).

Future Implications of Human Capital

With Southwest's success and reputation as an employer, you would think that people would stand in line to work for the company. You would be right. Recently Southwest Airlines opened a new hub in Oakland, California. The company needed to fill one hundred ground crew positions. The ground crew are the people who take your tickets and load and unload your baggage. No experience or specific education is required for these jobs. More than six thousand applicants showed up on the first day. More than nine thousand applicants showed up during the one-week interview period. Situations like this are not surprising given Southwest's reputation. What is surprising is that Southwest was able to fill fewer than half of the one hundred positions advertised.

HPT can have a tremendous impact on human capital. It can provide the management team with a system for effectively managing this form of capital. Will management be interested? Our experience indicates that management will eagerly welcome solutions to help it deal with its human capital problems. As we'll see in future chapters, the returns from improving performance can be quite substantial—so substantial that they will rapidly capture the attention and imagination of senior management.

You may be wondering why the issue of getting management on board appears so early in our book. After all, we haven't even told you yet how to develop a plan for implementing human performance technology within your organization. The answer is simple. It takes a while for management to make the mental shift from looking to training as a ready and simple solution to taking a systematic approach to performance improvement. Part of the problem is the vast array of "solutions" that managers have been bombarded with in the past twenty years. Consultants have come and gone with "*The* Answer to Management's Problems." Some of the proposed solutions have been adapted by management with varying degrees of positive impact on their organizations. Other solutions have either had a neutral impact or a negative one. Thus many managers have become skeptical of any new approach. Here is a partial list of what they have been sold during the past couple of decades (Pascale, 1991):

- Decision Trees
- Managerial Grids
- Satisfiers/Dissatisfiers
- Theory X and Theory Y

- Brainstorming

- T-Group Training

- Theory Z

- Conglomeration

- Management by Objectives

- Experience Curves

- Strategic Business Units

- Zero-Base Budgeting

- Value Chains

- Decentralization

- Wellness

- Quality Circles

- Total Quality Management (TQM)

- Excellence

- Restructuring/Delayering

- Portfolio Management

- MBWA

- Matrix Management

- Just In Time/Kanban

- Intrapreneuring

- Corporate Culture

- One-Minute Managing

- Benchmarking

- Cycle Time

- Visioning

- Workout

- Empowerment

- Continuous Improvement

- Learning Organization

- Business Process Reengineering

- Horizontal Organizations

- Core Competencies

- Self-Managing Teams

- 360 Feedback

After being subjected to all this, is it any wonder that managers are skeptical about proposed business panaceas? It will take some time to generate manager interest in the HPT approach to improving performance. You have a significant amount of work ahead and it will take some time to get management on board. Start now.

The Basics of Human Capital

Let's begin our human capital work with some basics, beginning with a clear definition of human capital. *Capital is assets used to generate gain*. Not all assets are capital. If I have a million dollars in my sock drawer, it's an asset, but it's not capital because it's not generating any gain. If I put the million dollars in a bank account to draw interest or if I invest it in the stock market, it now becomes capital. *Human capital is the people in an organization who are used to generate gain* (ideally this would be everybody on the payroll).

For example, Susan sells products to customers. She represents human capital to the organization. To the extent that we can improve her sales performance we increase her worth as human capital to the organization.

Human capital is different from intellectual capital. Intellectual capital is an asset that can be owned and controlled by the organization. Examples of intellectual capital include patents, databases of information, processes, and procedures. If an employee leaves the organization, the intellectual capital he or she created as an employee remains with the organization. However, human capital in the form of the departing employee himself or herself walks out the door and is a lost asset.

There are three fundamental aspects to managing human capital. All three must be done well to make the most of human capital and thereby create a competitive advantage for the organization.

1. Obtain the highest quality human capital possible: attract and hire the best possible people.

2. Keep human capital from leaving; it does you no good to hire the best if they leave soon after arriving.

3. Use human capital: optimize employee performance and contribution while they are in the organization.

HPT has a significant impact on all three of these fundamental aspects of managing human capital. This is why management will be so keenly interested in HPT once you make the connection for them. So let's get their attention by illustrating what's at risk through poor management of human capital.

Calculating the Cost of an Employee Asset, or They're More Expensive Than You Thought

How much does an employee cost? One's first reaction is probably to think about the salary cost of an employee on a monthly or yearly basis. But salary alone gives an incomplete picture. Employees cost more than just their salary expense, and most of them remain members of an organization for more than a month or a year. What is the real cost of an employee asset over the life of the asset, that is, over the term of his or her employment with the organization? Most managers will be very surprised to learn the answer, so surprised that they might well begin to think about managing human capital differently.

Let's examine how to determine the cost of an employee asset in your organization. First, you may want to talk with the financial controller for the organization or somebody from the finance department. The controller or finance department will have some numbers you will need and the consultation will add credibility to the process.

We start with the average yearly "fully loaded" cost of an employee, that is, the average yearly salary of an employee plus benefit costs, payroll taxes, occupancy, and so forth. The financial controller can tell you what cost factors are typically used in your organization. For our example we will set the average fully loaded cost as $100,000 per year. (Remember, they're not making that much; it's how much they're costing the organization.)

Next, we need to know how many years the organization will be experiencing the employee costs. The human resources department should be able to tell you what the average turnover rate is for your organization. Get out your calculator and divide 1.0 by this turnover rate. This will tell you how many years the average employee will be on the payroll. For our example, the turnover rate is 4 percent. This means that the average employee will be on the payroll for twenty-five years ($1.0 \div 0.04 = 25$).

The cost of employees will not remain steady at $100,000 for twenty-five years, of course. They will receive many raises during that period; other costs associated with employment in the company will increase as well. Ask the finance folks what the increase rate for your company is. In our example, we'll use a conservative yearly cost increase rate of 5 percent.

If you don't own a financial calculator yourself, find somebody who does (try finance again). If you are not familiar with financial calculators, somebody in finance should be able to help you. Take him out to lunch and ask him to bring his calculator. Here's how to calculate the cost of employee assets over the course of their asset life:

1. Use the Time Value of Money (TVM) function on the calculator.

2. Set the payments per year to 1.

3. For number of payments, enter the average number of years. In our example, this is 25.

4. For interest, enter the average yearly employee cost increase. In our example, this is 5 percent.

5. Enter 0 for the present value. (It would take pages to explain; just trust us on this.)

6. For payment, enter the average employee cost. In our example, this is $100,000.

7. Solve for future value.

The answer you get for your company's typical employee will probably surprise you. In our example, the cost of employees during their asset life is $4.77 million. Every employee in the organization represents an average $4.77 million asset. A manager of ten people is responsible for the care and maintenance of $47.7 million of company assets. Wow!

How do we use this information to build human capital awareness and prepare the management team for HPT? Well, consider the following scenario: Assume a manager in the organization is responsible for $47 million in capital machinery. The manager allows that machinery to be operated at 50 percent capacity. Would you consider him to be a good manager? What if he failed to invest in regular maintenance costs and allowed the machinery to fail and become useless to the organization?

The human capital parallels are obvious and the questions to management are compelling. What are we doing to remove barriers that prevent our $4.7 million assets from operating at peak effectiveness? What investments are we making in these assets to ensure that they retain their value over the course of their work lives? What is a reasonable investment to ensure that they retain their value? Present the data, raise the questions, and prepare for a lively discussion.

You now have management's attention. Let's go to the next step and calculate the cost of replacing existing staff.

The Cost of Replacing Human Capital

Many people believe that the loss of an employee is a minor, short-term inconvenience to the organization. The person leaves, a replacement is found who probably needs a little training, and the organization continues on course pretty much unchanged. Figure 3.1 illustrates this common perspective about employee turnover. The employee's value to the organization (productivity and performance) increases beginning the day he starts work and continues at a high level until he leaves the company. The organization experiences a small loss after his departure, manifested in a short dip in productivity. Then his replacement arrives, soon comes up to speed, and productivity goes back up again.

Unfortunately, the common view is simply unrealistic. It fails to look at the entire performance system as well as at the impact on the entire organization. Let's examine a more accurate model of what occurs when employees arrive at and depart from organizations. Figure 3.2 offers a more accurate and complete picture of the cost of replacing an employee.

A new employee arrives to start work at the organization. The organization experiences a net negative gain in productivity, as shown by area 1 in Figure 3.2. Why is this? Shouldn't the arrival of a new person boost the productivity of the organization? No. Ask yourself, What happens with new employees for the first couple of

Figure 3.1. Perceived Costs to Changing Employees.

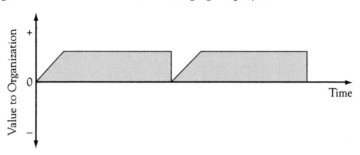

weeks? They spend significant amounts of time with their manager trying to get information about their job responsibilities. Meanwhile the manager has less time to attend to her other duties. New employees also turn to their coworkers for advice and help. Thus these coworkers spend time away from their usual duties training and mentoring the new employees. After a while the new employees become more capable and reach the break-even point; that is, their contributions finally match the time and effort the organization is investing in them.

As the new employees' capabilities increase, they become a net positive value to the organization. Area 2 in Figure 3.2 shows this positive contribution to the productivity of the organization, which continues on until something happens, such as the employee decides to leave the company.

What happens when an employee decides to leave an organization? Do her productivity and performance continue at their previously high levels? Of course not. When she decides to leave the organization her emotional commitment to the organization and her fellow employees, her dedication, and her effort decrease. Thus her performance level drops. Moreover, after she decides to leave the organization, she will most certainly spend company time working on her resume and calling colleagues at other organizations, spend personal time on interviews, and the like. This sudden and pronounced drop in productivity is indicated in Figure 3.2 in area

Figure 3.2. Realistic Costs to Changing Employees.

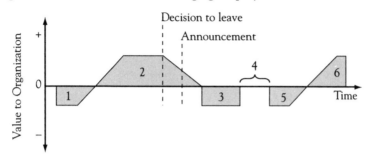

2 after the event labeled "Decision to leave." This lower performance will continue until the employee accepts a new position within the organization or with a new company.

Unfortunately, the bad news for the organization is not yet over. Once the employee announces an imminent departure, the net contribution to the organization drops even further. This is shown as the event labeled "Announcement" in Figure 3.2. Once the announcement is made, the employee has almost no motivation to perform. Time will be spent cleaning out the cubicle, and emotionally the employee will already be on the new job. Net contribution sinks to zero as the departing employee wastes the time of coworkers talking about the wonderful new job. The impact of influencing other employees to leave as well is not shown in the model but can be extreme.

When the employee finally departs, the organization experiences a significant net negative level of productivity. The human resources department (HRD) is busy searching for replacement candidates, managers are spending time in interviews and hiring discussions, and the remaining members of the organization are less productive as they juggle the responsibilities of their lost colleague. Area 3 in Figure 3.2 shows this productivity drop.

Once a replacement is hired, the organization returns to a net zero productivity gain for the employee position. This is represented by area 4 on Figure 3.2. This lasts for approximately two weeks while the organization awaits the arrival of the new team member. This zero productivity stretch could be much longer, based on the necessary capabilities necessary to fill the position and on the existing job market. If employee relocation is involved, the wait could easily run six to eight weeks, and even more for a foreign relocation.

When the new employee arrives, the organization experiences a net negative productivity, as shown by area 5 in Figure 3.2. The cycle has begun once again, with the new employee's contribution increasing over time until it reaches a net positive level represented by area 6, which continues until . . . well, you get the idea.

Why Do Employees Leave an Organization?

Given the costs that an organization experiences when an employee leaves, the reasons for such departures deserve consideration. People typically resist change. We like our set patterns and habits. What would cause people to leave their current job in search of another? Is there anything that can be done to keep them from wanting to leave?

Clearing Misconceptions

To understand why employees leave their jobs, we have to deal with a couple of pervasive misconceptions among managers and human resource professionals. The first misconception is that pay is the number one reason why people leave. Pay becomes a reason only if employees are paid far below the market value of their contributions. People typically will leave for a 40 percent pay increase, but not for a 10 percent increase. Very few people get a 40 percent pay increase when they change jobs. So why is the belief that pay drives the decision to change jobs so widespread? Because departing employees typically say that they are leaving because the new job offers more pay.

This brings us to the second misconception regarding why people leave their jobs. Managers and human resource professionals believe that departing employees will tell them the real reason they are leaving the organization. They don't. People are smart enough not to burn bridges behind them. If the new job doesn't work out, they may need to return to the old job. Pay is a safe reason for changing jobs, one that leaves the door open at the old job. Assume that a top performer leaves your organization. He cites pay as the reason. After two months he comes back, stating that money isn't everything, and that he has really missed his colleagues, the challenges of his old job, and the whole company. Would you take him back? Given a scarcity of top performers, you probably would.

Now assume that the same person leaves and is honest and candid about his reasons for leaving. He notes that he is tired of fighting the bureaucracy and frustrated by red tape and interdepartmental infighting that keep him from getting his work done. He also explains that he is disappointed in management's inability to create a stable strategy, so his work frequently is thrown away or redone. If he wanted to return, would you rehire him? Most likely not. So if pay is not the primary reason for leaving, what is?

Reasons for Leaving

Fredrick Hertzberg (1968) presented a model for employee motivation that is still in wide use within industry. Essentially he suggested that there are two categories of issues that affect how employees feel about their work and their job. First there are what he calls the *motivators*. These are the issues that bring joy to our work. Examples would be recognition, achievement, responsibility, advancement, and growth. The stronger the motivators, the greater our enthusiasm and satisfaction in our work.

Hertzberg calls his second group the *hygiene factors* or *dissatisfiers*. These are issues that people don't care about if they are done well but that can become a serious problem if left unattended. Policy and administration, supervision, work conditions, and salary are all hygiene factors.

Why do people really leave their jobs? It's typically due to a lack of motivators and/or a lack of attention to the dissatisfiers. It may be just one issue, such as a lack of opportunity to do meaningful work (achievement) or an unprofessional supervisor. It could also be a combination of factors. Some employees may be on the verge of quitting for years, turning in marginal performance due to a lack of motivation. The motivators and dissatisfiers need to be effectively managed to attract top human capital, optimize their performance, and keep them from leaving. HPT provides a system for accomplishing these goals.

HPT's Impact on Human Capital

Refer back to Chapter Two and our discussion of the human performance system (outlined in Figure 2.1). Human performance technology is a process that is focused on optimizing the human performance system by removing barriers to performance. By optimizing the performance of people in the organization, you are also effectively managing its human capital. The following two lists briefly explain how HPT affects the motivators and dissatisfiers that influence a person's decision to join or leave an organization.

Motivators

Achievement: If the performance system places barriers in the way of employees, their achievement will be decreased. HPT helps performers achieve more.

Recognition: HPT looks at the alignment between recognition of employee accomplishments and the organization's stated goals and expectations. Rewarding wrong performance and ignoring correct performance does not motivate employees.

Responsibility: People want to take ownership of their work and activities. HPT looks at organizational inputs (job requirements) to ensure clear objectives and performance charters.

Growth: Nobody wants to do the same job for twenty years. People want to grow. By removing barriers to performance, employees can spend less time overcoming obstacles, and more time developing themselves (increasing their human capital worth).

Dissatisfiers

Policy and administration: Nobody gets up in the morning and charges off to work because the organization has great policies and standards. If employees spend all their time overcoming bad policy and bureaucracy, however, they might want to work somewhere else. HPT looks at the policies and processes in which performers must work, and seeks to remove barriers.

Supervision: Managers are responsible for a great portion of the human performance system. They set the goals, control the rewards and recognition, provide feedback, and manage the work environment.

Work Conditions: From environmental factors to having the right tools, HPT looks at the conditions in which employees must perform, and seeks to change barriers into enablers.

In brief, HPT provides a significant tool for managing all three of the human capital factors: attracting high-quality people, optimizing their performance, and preventing them from leaving. These will be important points to bring out as you explain the potential value of HPT and human capital to management.

Finally, let's look at the last piece of data to use in our human capital discussions and presentations to management.

The Business Opportunity Costs of Mismanaging Human Capital

The turnover and suboptimization of human capital is more than annoying: it has a serious impact on the organization in terms of lost opportunity. To demonstrate this truth, we examine a concept known as *Break Even Time* (BET). Any project, whether targeted to produce a product, to develop a service, to effect an internal improvement, or whatever, takes time and involves costs. This investment yields benefits in terms of sales of a new product or reduced operating costs. Hopefully the benefit is greater than the costs. Figure 3.3 shows a typical BET analysis. In this example the organization experiences negative value for a period as it invests in the development of a new product. When the new product is introduced, it provides positive value to the organization until obsolescence. The obsolescence point is typically fixed, caused by market competition and innovation.

Figure 3.3 shows that the value outweighs the costs. But now let's assume that the organization is not managing its human capital very well. The organization is spending significant amounts of time dealing with turnover, and performance barriers are hampering employees. Will that product introduce on time? No. With suboptimized employee performance, the product will not be out as early as it could be. Product development delay occurs because employees are wasting time and energy overcoming performance barriers rather than developing the product. Figure 3.4 shows what happens when there is a delay due to poor human capital management. Costs increase and value decreases as a consequence.

The investment may be an internal process improvement. The human capital impact can be similar. If there are significant performance barriers in the organization, there will be limited time

Figure 3.3. The Break-Even-Time (BET) Model.

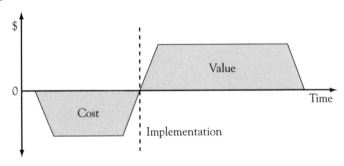

to implement new processes. The implementation of cost-saving changes can be significantly delayed. Figure 3.5 shows this impact. You can see that value is reduced due to the delayed implementation.

Create a Compelling Presentation on Human Capital and HPT

Management should be keenly interested in these human capital issues. Review this chapter and begin assembling the points and issues that weigh most heavily on management's mind. Be sure to help them understand the transition from training to performance when you are talking about the value of human capital and how it should be managed. You might want to bring up the issue of inability to take advantage of market opportunities because the organization was tied up spending time and money on unnecessary training. How much money has the organization thrown away on training that didn't make a difference?

We have found that providing managers with case examples as illustrations helps them to make the mental transition to understanding the importance of managing human capital and how HPT can help with the process. Case examples are always very persuasive, even if they don't come from within your own company or industry (like the Southwest Airlines example). They can effectively demonstrate the human capital point.

Figure 3.4. BET with an Introduction Delay.

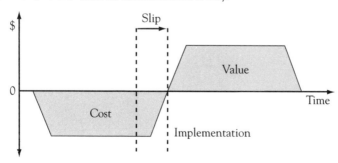

Figure 3.5. BET with a Slowed Implementation.

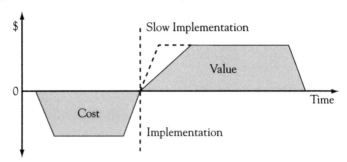

Summary: The Human Capital Message

Human capital is in short supply and getting scarcer. Organizations are finding that they cannot accommodate growth with their current hiring strategy. There's a shortage of qualified, capable human capital. This means that organizations must make the best use of the human capital they already have. They must make appropriate and effective investments in their employees' development. They must prevent the human capital from leaving the organization. The organization must remove barriers to effective utilization of its human capital. HPT is the best available methodology for doing this. Your job is to convince top management. This chapter is your resource for developing an effective presentation.

4

Preparing for Performance Technology

Our first three chapters have helped you (we hope!) to develop a clear and consistent understanding of performance technology. This chapter introduces you to the process of rolling up your sleeves and beginning the transition to HPT. There are a great number of transition issues to deal with. Where will your first projects come from? How will you fund performance technology? Who will be the first performance technologists? Where do you begin? In this chapter we begin by introducing the four phases of a planned approach to implementing human performance technology process in organizations and by reviewing the first phase in detail.

Planning to Make Changes

Before you begin the practice of HPT in your organization, it will be important to step back and take a look at where you are planning to go, what change issues should be taken into account, and how you are going to approach making these changes.

Getting Started

We offer a strong recommendation for beginning the transition to HPT: Start where you are and work methodically toward an organization-wide implementation. Do not attempt to convert the entire organization all at once: you will have neither the capacity nor the capability to implement many projects in the early stages of HPT adoption. The performance technology methodology will be viewed as a failure if you create a high level of excitement but then fail to deliver results (Kleiner, 1996). In addition, there may be significant organizational resistance to adopting HPT across the entire organization. Your plan should be to begin small, build capability, and demonstrate results. Successful results are a powerful tool to decrease resistance (Martin, 1995).

A quiet, grassroots approach has been shown to be highly effective in large organizations (Fuller, 1998; Ries and Trout, 1986) and even more powerful in smaller organizations. Small, limited pilot projects are best run by using existing resources or through very limited hiring. Results are measured and used to demonstrate the efficacy of the methodology. This approach will encourage organizational openness to HPT and enable you to take on larger and more visible projects. In time, HPT will be acknowledged as highly successful and vital to the future of the organization.

HPT Is an Organizational Change Issue

We need to recognize and acknowledge that HPT represents a significant change for the organization and eventually touches a wide range of personnel. People will no longer just "go to training." The role of the line business manager in improving performance changes considerably. Different parts of the organization will need to be involved in creating solutions to remove performance barriers. To be successful, an organizational change this extensive requires a carefully planned approach (Conner, 1993).

The process of organizational change is a defined practice. Several key factors must be addressed to increase the probability of success in making the change (Greenberg, 1994):

- The goal or end state must be well defined, so that the organization knows where it is headed.

- A plan for implementing the change strategy must be developed.

- Strong sponsorship is required to initiate and sustain the change.

- Communication about the changes must be clear and proactive.

- Some level of change resistance must be anticipated and resolved.

The Need for a Well-Planned Approach to Implementing HPT

Obviously, with so many change management issues to consider, the transition to HPT requires both general planning and attention to specific details. To take a haphazard approach to the transition from training to performance is to invite resistance, delays, confusion, and potentially the rejection of HPT entirely (Galpin, 1996). This book advocates a planned approach that we have used to start small and build to larger success within an organization. The phases of this planned approach are as follows:

1. *Prepare for performance technology by building capability and gathering resources.* This phase is addressed in this chapter.

2. *Demonstrate results.* Begin by implementing small projects that have a clear positive impact on the organization's business needs (cost, quality, quantity, and timeliness). Chapter Five outlines the plan for making this happen.

3. *Build organizational awareness.* With positive results in hand, begin to create awareness of HPT and its ability to achieve results. In Chapter Six you'll find specific recommendations on building awareness.

4. *Address the barriers to implementation.* As HPT becomes more broadly embraced, begin to address the organization-wide barriers to implementation. Chapter Seven focuses on helping to identify and address such barriers.

The Preparation Phase

Preparing for implementation is the first phase of the transition to HPT within your organization and the focus of the remainder of this chapter. During the preparation phase you quietly do work in the background before you begin to publicly promote HPT as the preferred method to improve performance within the organization.

There are several issues that you will need to address during the preparation stage. Who will act as the advocate or sponsor for developing HPT as a practice within the organization? Is there a shared understanding within your organization concerning what HPT is and isn't? Which HPT model will you use? Who will actually do the early HPT projects? What capabilities will they need? If you are the advocate for HPT, what capabilities should you be developing?

Now let's work through the preparation phase.

Step 1: Building Strategic Support Within the Organization

During this quiet stage of preparing for HPT implementation, you will want to begin building strategic support within the organization. Successful organizational change requires strong sponsors (Conner, 1993), and so do performance improvement projects (Fuller, 1997). The objective at this early stage is not to attempt to win over the organization's entire business management team. Rather, the objective is to find one or two strategic managers who will support the implementation of a few HPT pilot projects so that you can solve performance problems and demonstrate results within the organization.

The selection of sponsors is very important. They should be positioned high enough in the organizational hierarchy to be viewed as credible and powerful. However, choosing a sponsor who is too high in the organization may cause problems. You may receive a directive to implement HPT more extensively than the organization is ready for at this early stage. This places you in the difficult position of attempting to transform the entire organization at once, with no proven ability. Typically we have found that choosing a sponsor who is one or two levels above you on the organization chart is sufficient to begin with.

In addition to being at the right level, the sponsor should be prepared to fulfill his or her role. Remember that the sponsor's job is to provide permission for the implementation of the first few HPT projects. The sponsor may want or need to fund the initial pilot projects. You may also need to call on the sponsor to use his or her position power to remove roadblocks from the pilot team's efforts. For example, if you need data from the human resources department and the head of that department is not cooperating, you would want your sponsor to intercede for you with the human resource manager to help get your project back on track.

Step 2: Defining HPT for the Organization

If you are trying to move a team forward toward a goal, it is crucial that all the players on the team agree on what that goal is (Pritchett, 1991; Robbins, 1997). If the early HPT team can't agree about what HPT is, the organization as a whole probably won't be able to agree about it either. This becomes a significant barrier later, during the organization-wide implementation. If there are feuding HPT factions within the organization, management will frequently wait until there is agreement before proceeding with the implementation (Martin, 1995). An organizational change of this scope requires a clear, concise, and easily understood definition of the goal state (HPT) in order to succeed (Champy, 1995).

The definition that you select for your organization may be an existing one that you simply adopt and use. Or you may start with an existing definition and adapt it to suit yourself. Finally, you may elect to create a definition from scratch, that is, one written specifically for your organization that reflects language and cultural issues specific to that organization. In any case, this book serves as a valuable resource for choosing or developing a single definition of HPT for your organization.

In our experience, some organizations have found it useful to create two definitions for managing the transition to HPT. The first is a detailed, usually lengthy description of what HPT is and is not. This is typically used only within the HPT team to help the members keep themselves focused and aligned. The detailed definition and its documentation should never be widely distributed as a comprehensive description of what the organization does, for it would only confuse your clients or customers about the service you are offering. Avoid this pitfall. The HPT team will have the need, as well as the time and the patience, to read, study, and continually improve the detailed, internal document over time. Others will not.

The second definition, intended for general distribution, should be short and to the point. Sales experts have long promoted the use of the "thirty-second elevator pitch" to explain a product or service to an uninformed customer (Beckwith, 1997; Ries and Trout, 1986). Successful salesmen believe that if you can't describe a product or service during a thirty-second elevator ride, your description is too elaborate and confusing. You'll never capture the potential customer's attention and interest. The same is true for HPT. When a manager asks about "this HPT stuff," he or she is probably not looking for an hour-long presentation complete with charts and handouts. You should prepare a "thirty-second pitch" that will provide anyone with a quick and easily understandable general picture of HPT. Ideally this pitch should whet that person's curiosity about HPT and prompt him to want to find out more.

When the executive vice president of operations for the organization suddenly asks you what you're up to, you will be in a high-stress situation. You won't have time to work up a good thirty-second pitch. So practice your pitch before you'll need to use it. Test your thirty-second description with a variety of people who know nothing about HPT. Do they seem to get a clear picture of what you do? Do they ask you interesting and engaging questions to gather more information? Work on your HPT pitch until you can do it perfectly, even under stress.

Step 3: Selecting a Single HPT Model for the Organization

If creating a single definition of HPT is important, selecting a single HPT model is critical. The issue of HPT models is fiercely debated within the field. One side argues that having a rich collection of models allows an organization to be more adaptable to the needs of different performance improvement projects. It allows them to apply different kinds of model to different kinds of performance improvement projects. The other side advocates a single model, arguing that having a single model allows an organization to engage in continuous improvement of the HPT process and its implementation. Both sides in the debate are probably correct to some extent, but because of communication and consistency issues in the early stage of transitioning to HPT, we stress the need for a single model.

The HPT model serves as a major communication vehicle for the HPT team and its efforts. Because of its graphical nature, it tends to be remembered and recognized more readily than verbal description or documents about HPT (Tufte, 1990). Having multiple models floating around the organization does not lead to consistent and well-understood communication. By having multiple models, you are giving up brand-name recognition and logo identity, two major factors in establishing awareness (Beckwith, 1997).

Another danger with having multiple models within the organization is that different groups of individuals begin to gravitate toward different models and express a preference for one over another. This inevitably leads to some level of "model battles" where people take sides. Managers are bombarded with new books, methods, and models every day. As we discussed in Chapter Two, many of these proposed approaches to improving business have simply not worked, and managers are becoming wary of new approaches (Pascale, 1991). This problem is heightened if there is disagreement within the organization about the implementation of a new approach. Managers have been known to take no action on proposals until there is one model and consistent agreement about how the organization will use it (Champy, 1995). This is a delay to implementing HPT that you will want to avoid. Do the up-front work and select/create a single model from the beginning. Additional models can be brought in for consideration and use after your HPT program is well established within the organization.

When you select or create your HPT model, be certain that it accurately conveys how you intend to approach performance improvement projects. Your model must contain all the necessary elements to achieve a reliable and systematic approach to diagnosing the true causes of performance gaps. In general, the model should include the following:

1. Beginning with the business need of the organization
2. Determining the necessary performance to achieve the business need
3. Establishing the performance gap or gaps
4. Determining the root cause or causes of the performance gap or gaps
5. Selecting and implementing appropriate solutions to remove the root causes
6. Measuring performance to validate that the selected solution achieved the business needs

Step 4: Dealing with Initial HPT Staffing Issues

Another benefit of starting small and building on success is that you do not need to hire and/or create a large staff of HPT professionals all at once. Finding an experienced HPT practitioner is difficult. Finding a staff of them is almost impossible. U.S. graduate universities are producing less than four hundred instructional design/performance technology graduates per year (Ely and Minor, 1994) and they are in great demand. By starting small and gradually building large, you can extend the time available for locating or developing HPT staff. There is an added benefit to this method: by starting with a few resources, you typically do not need to engage in a long and painful funding discussion. If you are starting the HPT transition from within a large training department, there are typically one or two resources that can be redirected to early HPT work without a great deal of discussion (and sometimes no discussion at all).

Extreme care should be used in selecting the first few HPT practitioners. Their capabilities can greatly affect the success of the pilot projects. If you do not have obvious well-rounded candidates for the initial HPT positions, you will need to develop your human performance technologists during this preparation stage of the transition. Potential candidates within the organization typically have backgrounds that are strong in either systems thinking or people development. If you must choose between the two, select the candidates with the systems thinking backgrounds. Experience indicates that people development skills can be acquired faster than the systems thinking discipline (Fuller, 1998). If you need to locate potential candidates with strong systems thinking backgrounds, try looking in the quality or engineering functions within your organizations. You may be surprised how rapidly they can learn to apply their skills in systems thinking, problem analysis, root cause analysis, troubleshooting, and measurement to human performance systems.

Step 5: Developing the Early HPT Skill Needs

Stolovitch, Keeps, and Rodrigue (1995) wrote the authoritative article on the skill sets necessary to be an effective performance technologist. If you do not have a copy of the article, get it and read it. The authors identify sixteen key areas that must be in place for a mature performance technologist to be successful in the field; these areas include conducting needs analyses, specifying performance improvement strategies, evaluating interventions, and managing performance improvement projects. However, this does not mean that HPT work must wait until all the human performance technologists in the organization have fully mastered all sixteen skills. The article describes the goal and direction for the development of performance technologists.

To prepare for first HPT projects, you should be focused on core abilities that will allow the performance technologists to implement the HPT model you have selected. This will generally mean that you should focus early performance technologist development activities on the following areas:

1. *Understanding the business.* Do the performance technologists understand the business the organization is in, and can they construct a functional block diagram of the functions and processes of the organization? Do they understand how making a change in one part of the organization will effect the other parts of the organization? Do they understand how performance problems in one area can be caused by other departments in the organization?

2. *Understanding the process.* Can the performance technologists really implement the HPT process, and can they systematically apply it to eliminate performance barriers?

3. *Systems analysis skills.* Can the performance technologists conduct a root cause analysis to identify the true causes of the performance barriers? If not, do they have access to resources that can help?

Step 6: Developing the Skills of the HPT Advocate

We have already mentioned that if the transition to HPT is to be successful, it will need to have a strong advocate (Galpin, 1996). The advocate is responsible for maintaining a high level of awareness and excitement around the HPT process and projects. An advocate can offload the time-consuming responsibility for program communications and presentations from the still-developing HPT practitioners. The advocate will eventually be in the position of attempting to convince potential project sponsors to let the team analyze performance needs before creating solutions that seem obvious to the sponsor.

To properly fill this position, the advocate will need to be strong in several areas. As the success of HPT grows within the organization, presentations will need to be made. If the selected advocate (perhaps you yourself) has only average presentation skills, it's time for him or her to start developing superior capabilities now. During such presentations, questions about HPT methodology and its relationship to other management approaches will surely arise. The advocate should have a strong understanding of HPT fundamentals. Encourage him or her to read this book and *Human Competence* (Gilbert, 1996) now. Because HPT affects multifunctional processes, the advocate should learn more about all the parts of the business and initiate relationships with managers in different functional areas. To gain permission to use the HPT approach, the advocate should begin developing sales skills. Many have been successful just by asking somebody in the sales department for help. Try it.

Summary

In this chapter we have looked at the process for beginning the transition from training to performance improvement. We have made some specific recommendations regarding how to proceed:

- Start where you are and plan on moving methodically toward organization-wide implementation. Don't go for the big win all at once.

- Never promise more than you can deliver in the early stages.

- The implementation of HPT is an organizational change issue, and must be carefully planned if it is to be successful.

- Don't underinvest in preparation.

- Build organizational support for a "pilot status" for HPT.

- Create or select a single definition and model for HPT now, before it's too late.

- Start your staffing selection and development efforts now. You're already late.

- Make sure that you have a strong HPT advocate in place, or your performance technologists will spend their time on the wrong activities.

In the next chapter we move on to obtaining results based on preparation work that has been well planned and implemented.

5

Demonstrating Results with HPT

After diligently preparing for the transition to HPT and completing the first phase of the process, you are ready for the second phase of the transition: demonstrating that HPT has an impact on business results.

As we noted in Chapter Four, you may already have a sponsor who has agreed to support the HPT process. If not, however, you may have to sell HPT to your organization as well as find a client. In this chapter we help you look at the following:

- Criteria for selecting your first project

- Alternative ways to sell HPT: the hard-sell and the soft-sell approaches

- Ways to capture results: methods for getting quick results data, as well as more detailed methods.

Demonstrating HPT results is a difficult task, for you face a bit of a dilemma: your organization is not likely to share your enthusiasm for HPT. The organization has not seen the positive results of a performance improvement project and HPT has not been proven to work in your organization. You can't prove that it works until you have a chance to implement it. So the question becomes how to implement HPT before you have results to demonstrate that HPT actually works.

We are all familiar with the "head-on" or "hard-sell" sales approach, in which the person is attempting to sell us on something we are not sure we want. He simply persists in selling the benefits of his service or product in hopes that we will eventually say yes. This is a highly confrontational method, one that has mixed results. There is a method for securing permission to take an HPT approach to a project without having to do it head-on. Managers are frequently asking for help and some will be open to a different approach. This is where we will begin.

Once you begin to implement performance improvement projects, you will want to capture the results to demonstrate the impact that HPT can have on improving organization results. We discuss methods for obtaining quick results data, as well as more detailed and widely accepted methods.

Selecting Initial HPT Projects

If your organization is like most businesses, you will have a difficult time determining where to start because there are so many obvious opportunities for improving performance. Selecting initial HPT projects is an important issue. In addition to improving the performance of the organization, initial projects serve other purposes. First, they provide an opportunity to demonstrate the effectiveness and efficiency of using HPT. Second, the positive results of these projects serve as future sales tools for promoting HPT within the organization. Third, initial projects will likely provide your performance technologists with their first opportunity to practice their developing skills. Therefore the selection of initial projects needs to balance all three needs: achieving performance improvement, getting measurable results rapidly, and providing a somewhat safe learning experience for the new performance technologists.

You should be on the alert not to be seduced by the opportunity to achieve the "big win." There may be opportunities in the early stages of initiating HPT to engage in a large, highly visible, complex, politically charged project, for example, reengineering the manufacturing function within the organization. While achieving success in a project of this magnitude would move the transition to HPT forward by a great leap, a grand project is a poor place to start. It will take too long to achieve measurable results, it will certainly arouse significant resistance to taking the HPT approach, and your performance technologists won't have sufficient experience to deal with the complexities of the project. Let the big project pass and focus instead on appropriate smaller projects that will move HPT forward within the organization.

If you are developing an HPT team from the training organization, you have a ready-made lead generator for potential projects. Managers have learned that they can bring performance problems to the training group and get solutions. Begin by reviewing managers' requests for help. Then select a request that is well contained, that appears to be neither too large nor too difficult, and that has a manager/sponsor who is eager to get some rapid results.

Selling HPT to Your Organization

In this next section we discuss the pitfalls of taking an aggressive, head-on sales approach to promoting HPT in your organization. Then we explain the benefits of using an indirect approach.

The Head-On HPT Sales Method and Why It Doesn't Work

When you try to sell customers a product or service, they will typically want some assurance that the solution will work, meet their needs, and make them successful and happy (Beckwith, 1997). In the first stage of transitioning to HPT you will have no evidence to demonstrate that HPT will work in your organization, no success stories to tell, no testimonials to cite, and no financial analysis to prove that taking the HPT approach will make the project sponsor more successful. You are in the unenviable position of attempting to sell a product that the customer can neither touch nor see, that comes with no guarantees, that has no demonstrated success, and that is only vaguely understood (if understood at all) by the customer—who, by the way, has not even asked for it. Simply stated, this is not the optimal sales situation.

Unless you possess clearly superior sales capabilities, taking a head-on sales approach will almost certainly not result in winning permission to use the HPT approach to address performance improvement needs within the organization (Fuller, 1998; Ries and Trout, 1986). Training is the safe and established route for fixing performance problems. Few managers have ever been punished or even criticized for training their employees, even when it's not clear that they really need it. You will likely need to take a less direct sales approach to obtain permission to proceed with your first few projects.

The Indirect Method of Seeking Permission to Use an HPT Approach

There is an alternative to using the confrontational sales approach to obtain permission to put HPT into practice: *Don't bother to ask.* When a manager requests a training course, we typically don't feel the need to explain instructional systems design theory to ensure that she understands exactly how we are going to proceed with the development of the solution to her problem. Why should HPT be any different? As she explains her situation, simply agree to help her with her problem. She has come to you for help and you can promise to provide it in improving performance in her department.

Unfortunately, most managers do not explain their real problems in full detail. They typically come requesting a training course on a particular topic. They have already jumped from observing some performance "symptoms" to selecting a "cure" for that illness: more training. As the performance consultant, it is up to you to engage the manager in a dialogue that uncovers her real goal in asking you for the training course. Her real goal may be to reduce costs, to increase the quantity of work flowing through her department, to maximize timeliness of response to market conditions or customer needs, or to improve the quality of her department's work.

As you discuss the problem with the manager, you will want to identify the project success criteria. What specific goal does this manager have in mind? How will she know when the project is a success? Does she want to reduce manufacturing costs by 15 percent? Increase sales of Product X by 30 percent? Or get new products out on schedule? By establishing the manager's goal in this early stage, you are working in the first phase of the HPT process by identifying business needs. You are also identifying the evaluation criteria for the project.

You will need to secure permission to engage with the manager's organization to conduct the performance analysis. You can explain that to create an effective solution you would like permission to take a few days to talk with some members of her organization to understand what needs to be included and not included in the solution. You don't want to waste her organization's time with content that is unnecessary, nor do you want to leave out anything critical that would prevent the solution from working. Commit to getting back to her soon with your results. The results of your performance analysis will be one of the following:

- You agree that the requested training is necessary. You tell the manager that you know exactly what needs to be included in the training course for it to be efficient and successful (good news).

- You identify exactly what needs to be included in the training, but you also identify nontraining issues that need to be resolved if the training is to be effective (also good news, as you are preventing the manager from making a training investment that would not work).

- You find that training isn't the solution to her problem. Rather, you discover some nontraining issues that can

be fixed without having to take people away from their
jobs to attend training (typically really good news, as
the nontraining solutions can be put in place faster
and cheaper than the originally requested training).

This approach may appear rather daunting on first view. However, with a little practice the right words will flow easily from your
mouth. Here is an example dialogue between a manager, Sarah,
and a performance consultant, Shawn, that demonstrates how to
transform a training request into permission to take an HPT
approach on the project. Sarah is the general manager in a business unit within a medium-sized corporation. She has just sent a
memo to Shawn, who works in the training department and is
attempting to implement HPT. Sarah's memo indicates that she
wants a two-day training class on project management for all the
high-level business professionals in the organization (about 1,100
people). Her memo has asked Shawn to drop by as soon as possible to discuss the issue.

SHAWN: Sarah, you wanted to talk with me about some training.
Is this still a good time?
SARAH: Oh, sure, Shawn. Come on in and take a seat. You obviously got the memo so you know that I want to train up the
organization on project management. My big questions are how
much this will cost and how soon we can get started.
SHAWN: Sarah, I'd be glad to help you with this but I can give
you better answers if I know a bit more about the problem. I
know that you are a results-oriented manager and that you
would not send the organization off for two days of training
without a specific goal in mind. Could you describe what you
hope will be different in the organization as a result of this effort?
SARAH: Sure. I'm tired of our new products getting introduced
late and costing more than projected. Getting to the marketplace late and with high costs is no way to run a business.

SHAWN: So as a result of this project, new products should introduce on schedule and their costs should meet original projections. Is that right?

SARAH: Yeah, that's my hope.

SHAWN: Do we know what percentage of our new products have
introduced late and how badly over costs we are running?

SARAH: Well, you can check with accounting to get the exact
figures. We track all that information. But off the top of my head
I'd say that all the products have been at least a month late and
are running about 8 percent over original costs.

SHAWN: Sarah, to ensure that you get a solution that meets your
business needs, I'd like to figure out what needs to be included
to make it work. You don't want to waste time on content that
isn't needed and you don't want to do it twice because something got left out.

SARAH: OK.

SHAWN: I'd like to take a few days and talk with some of the
folks in your organization to ensure that we create a solution
that really helps you achieve your objectives. I'll be back in a
few days to let you know what I have found.

SARAH: OK, but don't keep me waiting long. Time is money!

The next week Shawn returned with the results of his performance analysis.

SHAWN: Sarah, still a good time?

SARAH: Yes. I have been eager to find out what you discovered.

SHAWN: I think that I have pretty good news. Most of the organization has a strong understanding of project management fundamentals and they seem able to implement most of the process. It doesn't
look like they need the two days of project management training.

SARAH: Then why are the projects late?

SHAWN: That was my question. What I found out in talking with
the project managers and reviewing a few project results is that

each function, like marketing or R&D, does a great job of managing their portion of the project. The problem comes during the transfer from one function to another. There seem to be delays because deliverables don't meet specs and there is no formal communication process. As a result, the transfer gets fumbled, injecting additional time into the process. We have identified a process and a communications tool to help with the transfer phase. Folks will need about half a day of workshop time to learn how to put them to use.

SARAH: What about the cost overruns?

SHAWN: Another interesting issue. It turns out that the finance manager is not very supportive of her staff being tied up in project planning meetings. As a result, the R&D team must make the first-pass cost estimates on their own. It's not something they do very well. Finance doesn't seem to get involved until well into the project, when many of the cost issues are already decided and unchangeable. You simply need to get finance into the projects earlier.

SARAH: I'll call the finance manager this afternoon. How soon can the project transfer workshops begin?

SHAWN: We have identified a vendor who can start in two weeks. Here's the cost projection.

SARAH: Well, it's certainly less than I planned to pay for the two-day training. Nice work, Shawn.

Taking this more subtle approach avoids the unnecessary process of attempting to educate the client on the philosophy, process, and practice of HPT. Sarah came to Shawn in search of a solution to her performance problem. Shawn got clarification on the issue, sought permission to look into the problem, identified the root causes, and proposed workable solutions. Sarah is obviously happy with the initial results, and she may come back to find out more about the approach Shawn took. An interested and curious sponsor is a better audience for an HPT sales talk than a manager who is confronted by someone using the head-on sales technique. The results of early HPT projects will generate interest and open the door for further discussion and explanation of the process that you used.

Capturing Early HPT Project Results

After you have completed your first HPT projects, you will want to continue the effort of measuring the results of improved performance. These results are an important tool in transitioning the organization to HPT. During the transition from training to performance most organizations struggle with the issue of how best to measure the effectiveness of the performance improvement projects. Initially, it may seem like an enormous process, requiring tremendous amounts of time and effort. Several issues typically come to mind when thinking about implementing an evaluation strategy:

- How can we get evaluation results quickly, rather than waiting six months to show the project's impact on the organization?

- What must be done to prove beyond a doubt that the performance improvement solutions caused the change in organizational performance?

- Who will gather the data and what data capture mechanisms will need to be designed?

- How can we work up to Level 4 evaluation results, which measure financial impact on the organization, when the experts say that it cannot be done?

These are all great questions and you can see why they would weigh heavily on the minds of the performance technologists. We will address each of them as we look at methods for measuring and evaluating the effectiveness of performance improvement projects. The methods we will look at are

1. Cost Avoidance

2. Time on Task

3. Return on Investment

Cost Avoidance

Definition: The cost avoidance measure looks at the cost savings represented by taking the HPT approach rather than the originally requested solution (usually training).

One of the issues regarding measuring the results of performance improvement projects is the time delay. To conduct a longitudinal before/after performance comparison requires time. This may significantly slow the HPT momentum that you are attempting to build. The solution is to take a progressive evaluation strategy for the first few HPT projects.

You can begin to measure HPT's contribution to the organization immediately after implementing performance improvement solutions. Chances are that the first project was initiated by a training request that you skillfully transformed into permission to take an HPT approach. Training is typically one of the most expensive performance improvement solutions that can be used. The costs of developing the training plus the costs of implementation can be quite high. It is also likely that the cost of the final performance improvement solution was less than the training that was originally requested. This represents immediate cost savings to the organization! Such savings are referred to as *cost avoidance*. It's not the best measurement but it's not a bad place to start when you want to show early results.

Begin by capturing the costs of fulfilling the original training request, including

- Development of the proposed training

- Implementation costs, including materials, facility, and instructor

- Instructor travel costs (if the training needs to be held in multiple locations)

- Cost of the employees attending the training (time and travel)

Compare the potential costs of the training that had been requested to the actual costs of the HPT project that you have just implemented. The HPT project will typically cost less than the training. If it is less, you can demonstrate bottom-line cost savings to the organization.

Here's an example. A manager requests that a three-day training class on customer satisfaction be given to all the field engineers in the company. Customers are complaining about service and selecting other companies to perform maintenance on installed equipment. The manager is adamant about fixing this problem.

The performance analysis indicated that field engineers were taking far longer than expected to perform maintenance and repair procedures. The customers were upset because they wanted their machinery up and running as soon as possible: while it was off-line they were losing money. The root cause of the field engineers' slow work was an inadequate supply of spare parts and other materials in their cars when they arrived at repair sites. After diagnosing the machine's problem, the engineer frequently had to drive back to the office for additional parts, which caused significant delays in the machinery repair process and further upset the customers. The solution to the performance problem was to increase the inventory of spare parts and other materials in the field engineers' cars. This cost approximately $650 for each of the eight hundred field engineers, or $520,000. The half-million dollars was not really a sunk cost. It was simply an increase in inventory, which is an asset. However, the organization did need to pay the half-million dollars to get the project rolling, so we'll treat it as a cost for this analysis.

Let's look at the cost of the original training request. The analysis is summarized in Exhibit 5.1. The manager requested an off-the-shelf customer satisfaction training course, so there were no development costs associated with the training course. A vendor was identified who could deliver the training to groups of twenty in the various sales areas across the United States. The vendor charged $12,000 per class, including instructor and materials. Instructors' travel was an extra cost, as were fees to rent training sites at hotels across the country. Field engineers would need to travel to these sites for their training, and this travel was also an expense of the training. But all this is just the tip of the iceberg of total training costs. Here is our training cost summary:

Solution development costs = $0

Solution implementation costs = $564,000

Total attendee costs = $10,036,000

Now we will explain how we calculated these costs. Let's look at the solution implementation costs first. The company employs eight hundred field engineers, who would be trained in groups of twenty. Thus the engineers would require forty classes. The training company will charge $12,000 for each class, so the classes would cost $480,000 (40 × $12,000). To this basic charge must be added the instructors' travel costs, estimated to be $24,000 for the different training locations. Moreover, the training must be held at hotel sites all over the country, at a cost of $500 per training day, or $60,000 (3 days per training session × 40 sessions × $500). Thus the total implementation costs for training would be $564,000.

Now let's look at attendee costs. Because almost every field engineer would need to travel to a central site, travel costs would not be small. According to the accounting department, seven hundred of the eight hundred field engineers would need to travel a significant distance to the training site and each of these seven

Exhibit 5.1. Training Cost Avoidance Calculation.

Calculation Method	Costs
Development Costs:	
Existing training course cost nothing to develop	$0
Implementation Costs:	
800 engineers/20 students per class = 40 classes needed	
40 classes × $12,000 per class = $480,000	$480,000
Instructor travel costs = $24,000 based on location of students	$24,000
Hotel rooms: 3-day class × 40 classes = 120 hotel days	
Hotel costs: $500 per day × 120 days = $60,000	$60,000
Total implementation costs	$564,000
Attendee Costs:	
700 engineers × average travel costs of $840 = $588,000	$588,000
100 engineers would not need to travel = $0	$0
Fully loaded cost of engineer = $16,000 per month	
Engineer cost of $16,000/21 working days = $762 per day	
800 engineers × 5 days (3 in class, 2 days traveling) = 4,000 days	
4,000 engineer days × $762 per day = $3,048,000	$3,048,000
Average engineer revenue = $1,600 per day	
800 engineers × 5 days × $1,600 = $6,400,000	$6,400,000
Total attendee costs	$6,400,000
Cost Avoidance Calculation:	
Cost of original proposal = Development costs + Implementation costs + Attendee costs = $0 + $564,000 + 10,036,000	$10,600,000
Subtract the cost of the Performance Improvement Solution	–$520,000
Total cost avoidance	$10,080,000

hundred would have an average travel cost of $840 for the three days, or $588,000. According to the finance group within the organization, the fully loaded cost of a field engineer (salary, taxes, benefits, overhead, use of a company car, and so on) is $16,000 per month. Because there are twenty-one working days in the average month, a "field engineer day" costs the organization $762 ($16,000 ÷ 21 = $762). Because each engineer would spend three days in class and two days traveling, these five days associated with the training would cost the company $3,048,000 (800 engineers × 5 days × $762/day = $3,048,000). In addition to the engineer costs per day, the company was losing out on revenue that the field engineers would normally have generated at work. According to our friends in finance, each engineer generates an average of $1,600 in revenue per day. Thus the eight hundred engineers would have generated a whopping $6,400,000 for the company had they not been traveling and taking the training classes (800 engineers × 5 days × $1,600 = $6,400,000). Thus total attendee costs, that is, both direct (for training, travel, and the like) and indirect (cost to the company in lost earnings, and so on), would have been $10,036,000. Most managers are not aware of this huge cost because it is spread across the organization and nobody has to sign for it.

The total cost for the proposed training would have been $564,000 in implementation costs plus $10,036,000 in attendee costs, for a total of $10,600,000. To determine the cost avoidance, we subtract the cost of the performance improvement solution, which was $520,000. This gives us a cost avoidance of $10,080,000. Not a bad result for two weeks of analysis work. Some managers might object to this accounting method. They might well argue that including field engineer costs and lost revenue is a form of double counting. Let's grant them this point and remove the field engineer costs from the equation. We would still have a cost avoidance of $7,032,000. Again, we had management's attention.

Time on Task

Definition: Time on task assesses impact by measuring the increased amount of time spent on tasks valued by the organization.

An intermediary measurement is "time on task" (Stolovitch, 1998). Many performance improvement projects seek to lower costs or increase results by removing time-wasting activities. If this is the case with your project, you can measure the percentage of time spent on desired tasks before and then a couple of weeks after the interventions are implemented. This will provide demonstrable, intermediary results while the data for the return-on-investment evaluation is being collected. Both cost-avoidance and time-on-task results can be effectively used to generate interest and confidence in the HPT method. The general formula for calculating time on task is shown in Exhibit 5.2.

To measure time-on-task value you will need several pieces of information, including the following:

1. The average percentage of time that is spent on the time-wasting activity prior to the implementation of the performance improvement solution

2. The average percentage of time that is spent on the time-wasting activity after the implementation of the performance improvement solution

3. The number of employees affected by the performance improvement solution

4. The cost of the time being wasted

When you look at percentage of time being spent, it can be viewed in two ways. You can either look at time spent on nonproductive tasks (for example, filling out forms, searching for information, driving back to the sales office) or conversely you can look at time spent on productive tasks. Either way, the before/after comparison should show a

Exhibit 5.2. Time-on-Task Formula.

1. Calculate the total amount of time spent unproductively before the intervention:
   Average time spent on nonproductive activity *before* the intervention
   × number of work days per year
   × number of performers
   = total unproductive time before intervention

2. Calculate the total amount of time spent unproductively after the intervention:
   Average time spent on nonproductive activity *after* the intervention
   × number of work days per year
   × number of performers
   = total unproductive time after intervention

3. Calculate the amount of unproductive time avoided:
   Average time spent on nonproductive activity *before* the intervention
   − average time spent on nonproductive activity *after* the intervention
   = total unproductive time avoided

4. Calculate the value of increased time on task:
   Total unproductive time avoided
   × average cost of performer time
   = value of increased time on task

decrease in nonproductive, time-consuming tasks and an increase in the time spent on productive tasks.

To capture time on productive or nonproductive tasks, you have several options. You can ask the performers in question, but this method typically generates unreliable results. People's opinions concerning how much time they spend on activities are usually not very accurate. You can take a "snapshot" survey, where you ask a large sample of performers to keep an accurate log of what they do during the course of the day in fifteen-minute increments. A one-week sample is typically adequate. With this method, compliance can sometimes be an issue, particularly if participants have doubts regarding how the information will be used. Another alternative is to do a random "ride-along" analysis. Pick a few performers at random, follow them around for the day, and log their activities. Whichever method you choose, be sure that the same performers are available for both the before and the after measurements.

To establish the cost of the time, I suggest that you work with the folks in the finance group in your organization. Even if you will be doing all the analysis, have the finance folks review your numbers to add confidence and reliability to your calculations. When looking at the cost of the time, you use what it costs the company to have the person working, including fully loaded overhead costs. This includes salary, taxes, benefits, occupancy, phone, and so on.

Looking back at the example of the field engineers, let's calculate the value of the performance improvement solution using time on task. The calculation is summarized in Exhibit 5.3.

During the performance analysis, we conducted several "ride-along" trips where we accompanied field engineers for the day. During the analysis, we made careful notes regarding how they spent their time. This provided us with a limited data sample, however. We compared the measured time with a number of time logs submitted by field engineers (they do this as a natural part of their job because billing is based on time spent working at the customer site). We also asked field engineers to estimate the amount of time they spent hunting down parts and materials. Our observations, the field logs, and the field engineer estimates were all very close to one another. We estimated the nonproductive time to average 1.67 hours per day.

We were able to use the same cost number from the cost-avoidance exercise. Because a field engineer costs an average of $762 per day, a "field engineer hour" is worth $95.

We waited two weeks after the additional parts and other materials were issued to the field engineers before collecting data on the results of our intervention. We wanted to allow sufficient time to ensure that all the engineers had been properly equipped and had settled into their new routine. Nonproductive time did not drop to zero. The field engineers still experienced situations in which they

Exhibit 5.3. Time-on-Task Calculation.

---

1. Calculate the total amount of time spent unproductively before the intervention:
Average time spent on nonproductive activity *before* the intervention
1.67 hours per day

× number of work days per year	232 days
× number of performers	800 engineers
= total unproductive time before intervention	309,952 hours

2. Calculate the total amount of time spent unproductively after the intervention:
Average time spent on nonproductive activity *after* the intervention
0.13 hours per day

× number of work days per year	232 days
× number of performers	800 engineers
= total unproductive time after intervention	24,128 hours

3. Calculate the amount of unproductive time avoided:
Average time spent on nonproductive activity *before* the intervention
309,952 hours
– average time spent on nonproductive activity *after* the intervention
24,128 hours

= total unproductive time avoided	285,824 hours

4. Calculate the value of increased time on task:

Total unproductive time avoided	285,824 hours
× average cost of performer time	$95 per hour
= value of increased time on task	$27,153,280

---

needed to go back to the sales office for parts or materials. However, the parts they needed were typically strange, unusual, or unpredictable (the part that breaks one in a thousand times). Using the same techniques and the same sample engineers, we found that their nonproductive time had dropped to an average of 0.13 hours per day.

Now we need to do the calculations. The performance intervention caused nonproductive time to drop from 1.67 to 0.13 hours, or a reduction of 1.54 hours per day. There are 232 working days in a year, after deducting weekends, vacation days, and holidays. Eight hundred engineers were affected by the performance solution.

$$1.54 \text{ hrs per day saved} \times \$95 \text{ per hour cost} \times$$
$$232 \text{ working days per year} \times 800 \text{ field engineers} = \$27,153,280$$

A large figure such as this certainly has the potential to capture management's attention. Recognize that this is not quite a cost saving to the organization yet. Costs are not going to drop $27 million; after all, the company is still paying the field engineers. However, the organization has just recaptured $27 million in lost time (for example, driving around in the car) and refocused it on productive activity (repairing and maintaining customer products). This is not a bad evaluation result to post just a few weeks after implementing the solution. It will keep management interested and enthused about HPT while you are working on the real bottom-line impact of the performance improvement project.

Return on Investment

Definition: Return on investment (ROI) measures the bottom-line impact (for example, reduced costs, increased revenue) compared with the cost of achieving the improvement.

Ultimately, you will want to demonstrate the bottom-line impact that the performance improvement project has had on the organization. How has product quality improved as a result of the performance interventions? How much have costs declined as a result? What are the incremental sales of product? Managers will be keenly interested in the answers to these kinds of questions.

At the beginning of this section we posed some difficult questions. It's time to start answering them. How can we work up to Level 4 evaluation results when the experts say that it cannot be done? You are probably familiar with Donald Kirkpatrick's *Evaluating Training Programs: The Four Levels* (Kirkpatrick, 1975). Level 4 is the measurement of impact on the organization. Level 4 is the most desirable level of measurement, but few projects are ever evaluated at this level due to the perceived difficulty of measuring the impact. However, the difficulty is an illusion based on the old perspective on performance improvement. It is very hard to get high-level evaluation results (like Level 4) when you begin with the solution (that is, training) and then search for a problem that needs fixing. "Linking training to business needs" is simply backward thinking. It is very difficult to establish that the solution had any impact on a change in performance.

HPT allows us to completely reverse the process of evaluation. Rather than attempting to link the solution to the problem, HPT starts with the problem and works toward the solution. You will find that your evaluation efforts begin at the start of the performance analysis. If you remember the process for performance analysis presented in Chapter Two (Figure 5.1 shows the basic performance technology model), it begins with identifying the business issue and the desired outcomes. Working forward in the process, the performance gaps are measured and the root causes of these gaps are identified. Based on the root causes, the performance improvement solutions are specifically selected. Therefore we have data that link each phase of the performance analysis process to the others. Decisions are made based on this data.

When we implement solutions, we are working backward through the performance analysis process (refer to Figure 5.1). We implement the solutions that remove the root causes, that close the performance gaps, that allow the organization to achieve the desired outcomes. The data that linked the phases as we moved forward through the process are the same data that link it as we move backward during implementation.

Now here is the breakthrough that the performance analysis process allows us. Rather than beginning with Level 1 evaluation (participant reaction), we can begin with Level 4 (impact on the organization results). Why? Because we have data that indicate that our solution will remove root cause barriers, close the performance gap, and allow the organization to achieve its identified business

Figure 5.1. Basic Performance Technology Model.

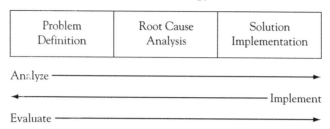

goal. We have data that indicate that the solution will have an impact on the goal, so we will begin our evaluation with the organizational outcome. If you refer to Figure 5.1, you'll see that we will evaluate starting at the highest level. If we achieve our Level 4 results, we can stop the evaluation process.

After establishing that we can begin our evaluation at Level 4, the next question typically has to do with data collection and management. Where are the resources going to come from? How do we establish the credibility of the data? How do we get management to buy into the measures? Although these questions may seem imposing, the answers are really quite easy. The work has probably already been done for you.

Refer back to the performance technology model discussed in Chapter Two (pictured in Figure 2.2). When we were identifying the business issue and the desired outcome, we were creating the foundation for the evaluation of the performance improvement project. The project sponsor indicates that there is a problem with sales of a new product and he states that he wants sales to increase by 30 percent. The project sponsor has just set the Level 4 evaluation goal for the project. As a result, what will be your measurement? Obviously, sales of the new product, with a goal of a 30 percent increase. The project sponsor will buy into this measure of success because he chose it.

Where are you going to get the resources to collect and manage the data? You don't need any. The organization is already collecting and managing the data for you. Management knew there was a performance problem because its own data indicated that sales of the new product were not meeting expectations. There is no need to establish credibility for this data because the organization itself collected sales data before and after the implementation of the performance intervention, and the organization won't question the credibility of its own data.

We can now proceed to measuring and reporting the results of your performance improvement project. After allowing the organization to continue to collect data for you, you can present a before/after evaluation of the performance improvement project. Simply chart the data over time and indicate where the organization implemented the performance improvement solutions. If the solution was a change of process or environment, the correlation between the intervention and the improved performance will be compelling. In the case of the field engineers, we saw results in under a week. Figure 5.2 illustrates what a results chart looks like. You can see the performance before and after the intervention occurs.

It's time for the first major objection. Can you prove beyond a shadow of a doubt that it was the performance improvement intervention, and only the intervention, that was responsible for the results? The answer to this question is simple: no, of course not. Fortunately, our audience for the evaluation results is not the U.S. Food and Drug Administration, who demand absolute proof. Our audience, the managers of the organization, is much more reasonable. You may in fact be asked this question the first time you present your results. Acknowledge that the chart you have constructed is not absolute proof but point out to your audience that the correlation is pretty compelling. Ask your audience to remember your presentation and tell them that you will be returning. After your second HPT pilot project is completed, address the management audience again. Again, you will show them a chart, similar to the one in Figure 5.3, illustrating the correlation between your intervention and the cost of manufacturing a product. Is your second

Figure 5.2. Results Chart Showing Impact of Performance Intervention.

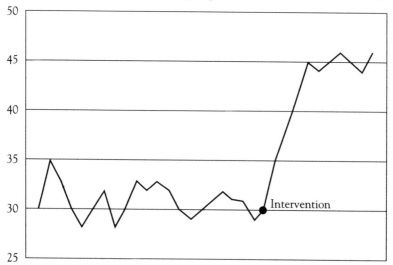

chart a more absolute proof than the first one was? No, but the cor-relation is more compelling now that you have two examples of suc-cess. Some formerly skeptical managers will be convinced. By the conclusion of the third successful intervention, with your third pre-sentation and third chart, there should be no naysayers or skeptics in your audience, and the effectiveness of HPT will be established.

Once the management team is convinced of HPT's effective-ness, you can move on to demonstrate the bottom-line ROI. If this is your first attempt at calculating the ROI for an HPT project, you may want to seek some assistance from your finance organization, at least to review your work and assumptions.

ROI measures the value of an investment compared with the cost of making the investment. The calculation is remarkably sim-ple. Take the value (return) of the investment and divide it by the cost of the investment. For example, if you bought a stock at $1 and sold it for $2, the value of the investment is $2 and the cost was $1. This gives you a ROI of 2:1 or 200 percent. You doubled your money. The difficulty in calculating the ROI is not the calculation

Figure 5.3. Results Chart Showing Cost Impact of Performance Intervention.

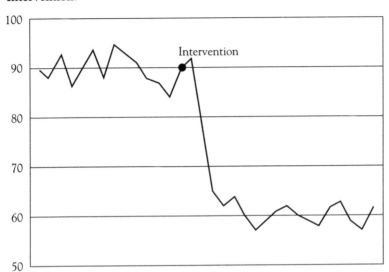

itself but determining a measure of the value (return) to the organization. We are going to make it easier.

Management has already selected the measure for success in terms of sales, quantity, or quality. By demonstrating the correlation between the intervention and the results, you have buy-in that the performance intervention was responsible for the change in performance. All you need to do is establish the return that the organization has received from the improved performance. You already know what the performance improvement solutions cost.

We begin by looking at our results chart. Figure 5.4 is a version of Figure 5.2 with some additional information. If we look at the chart, we can see that there were fairly consistent and predictable sales results in the organization. Sales were growing but not quickly. We can extrapolate what the sales would have been without the intervention, as indicated by the straight line that starts after the intervention. This sets a baseline for performance. We can now compare the actual performance with the expected performance

Figure 5.4. Results Chart Showing Return on Performance Intervention.

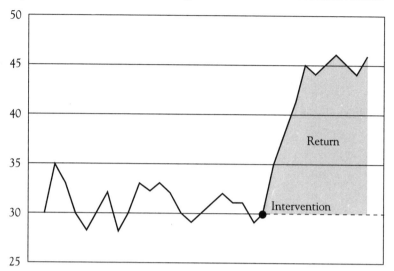

over time. The return to the organization is the area between the actual and the old expected performance. Add up the returns and divide that number by the cost of the intervention and you have your Level 4 ROI measurement.

Let's look at the ROI for the field engineers. We increased time on task by 1.54 hours per field engineer per day. By spending more time on task, each field engineer made more money for the company each day. Total revenues increased by over 20 percent with the same number of engineers. In other words, the intervention increased revenues by some $63 million. Now take this $63 million, divide it by $520,000 (the cost of the intervention), and the result is an ROI of 12:1 or 1,200 percent. After seeing these figures, management had very good reasons to become interested in future HPT projects.

Summary

In this chapter we have laid out an approach for obtaining results with early HPT projects. Some of the key points we made are as follows:

- Early projects must be carefully selected for size and complexity.

- Rather than taking a head-on sales approach, use a more subtle approach to secure permission to conduct the performance analysis.

- Establish measures for success at the beginning of the project.

- Plan to measure the effectiveness of the project using cost avoidance, time on task, and return on investment.

In the next chapter we look at how to take the results that you have achieved and use them to generate increased awareness of and interest in HPT.

6

Building Organizational
Awareness for HPT

W hile you are beginning to do human performance consulting within the organization and gathering data about your
results, you can also be building organizational awareness of this
new approach. Our experience has shown that just because you
have prepared your current staff or department to do performance
consulting does not mean that your customers will come knocking
on the door asking for help with some nontraining issue. For a long,
long time they will continue to ask, most of the time, for training
programs (or facilitation for off-sites, or whatever they are accustomed to getting from your staff). You will have to take some initiative and expend a considerable amount of effort toward creating
an awareness of HPT in your organization. People will need to learn
that they *can* ask you for help with analyzing and solving performance issues—and that there is a larger, more robust, and inclusive
way of looking at business problems than simply bringing in someone to teach a three-day course on "How to Fix This Annoying or
Costly Symptom."

Building awareness for HPT in your organization will require
some preparation on your part. At a minimum, you will need to prepare for three pivotal communications events:

1. Describing HPT in formal or informal settings with just a sentence or two

2. Selling HPT as a concept and a practice

3. Answering change management and political issues

Creating a Short, Clear Description

Not only do you need a clear description of HPT but you also need to be able to explain what HPT is in your own words, at any time, in almost any circumstance, in about thirty seconds. And after briefly describing HPT you must be prepared to answer an unpredictable stream of questions you may not have imagined and to address objections that range from the thoughtful to the cynical to the just plain misinformed. Given that less-than-encouraging introduction, you should mentally prepare to work hard, both on your own and with your staff, so that any member of your training team can consistently and reliably describe HPT to your own and to your clients' satisfaction. You'll know you are successful when you can clearly and accurately describe HPT to your company's CEO while sharing an elevator ride with him or while waiting next to her in the cafeteria line.

To create your own definition, it may help to start with one that someone else has written, for example: "HPT is a systemic and systematic approach to defining a business need or opportunity, identifying the barriers to achieving the desired business result, implementing solutions to remove the barriers to performance, and then measuring the bottom-line results." This is a long sentence that may cause the eyes (and minds) of most business managers to glaze over, but it provides us with a starting point. It can work well when projected on a slide during a presentation, when you can talk through each segment of it, but it won't work well in a short exchange by the coffee machine.

Let's take this definition apart in the hopes that doing so will encourage you to choose your own words that you can exchange for ours and use anytime, anywhere.

1. *HPT is a systemic and systematic approach to defining a business problem or opportunity.*

Part of the definition: "systemic."

Plain language: A way of looking at each element of a problem or opportunity as part of a system. Few parts of a problem or opportunity will ever exist in isolation. If you fix one thing, another may break. For example, if you concentrate on learning but ignore motivation, people may not do what you taught them to do. Every element in a problem or opportunity is related to several other elements, some of which may not be obvious at first glance.

Part of the definition: "systematic."

Plain language: Following a well-organized procedure, having a step-by-step approach. Having a method or system that is known for achieving results.

Part of the definition: "defining a business problem or opportunity."

Plain language: Making sure you know what the problem or opportunity is that you are trying to solve. Defining the problem or opportunity in business terms; usually this is quantified in terms of time, money, or quality.

2. *Identifying the barriers to achieving the desired business result.*

Part of the definition: "identifying the barriers."

Plain language: Figuring out the root cause of the problem or the real reason why an opportunity is not being realized. Making sure you go beyond the symptoms of what might be wrong or holding you back and getting to the real issues.

Part of the definition: "achieving the desired business result."

Plain language: Keeping in mind why you are trying to eliminate a particular barrier to performance. For example, a barrier might keep people from selling enough of your products to meet the company's goals.

3. *Implementing solutions to remove the barriers to performance.*

Part of the definition: "implementing solutions."

Plain language: Barriers can be eliminated by employing a variety of solutions. Some solutions address the environment in which people work, for example, providing the correct tools or reducing noise and distractions so that people can concentrate. Other solutions address motivational factors, for example, an incentive program that encourages the sales force to sell one product over another or a management strategy that helps people to see that they need to invest more effort to succeed with a particular task. A third type of solution has to do with knowledge and skills, for example, a lecture/lab training program to teach a new manufacturing support system or a web-based training program to update customer service representatives on software revisions. Finally, it will often take a combination of interventions to solve a business problem or to realize an opportunity.

Part of the definition: "to remove barriers to performance."

Plain language: None of the solutions implemented are created for their own sake, but rather to increase performance: lower costs, increase profits, hasten the timeline. Given that a variety of interventions may be necessary, it is important for the performance consultant to watch over the implementation of the various solutions to ensure that the barriers are, in fact, removed.

4. *Measuring the bottom-line results.*

Part of the definition: "measuring the bottom-line results."

Plain language: Making sure that the business goal was achieved by checking to see that the improvement in terms of time, money, quality, or some other measure was achieved. This goal would have been established during the first part of the process: defining the business problem or opportunity.

For your own definition, you might adopt some variation of something like this: "HPT is a way to figure out what really gets in the way of the results we're looking for and then to put solutions in place that will help us to achieve those results." It's a really great idea to practice your definition until it's perfect. Practice it on your friends and relatives and with people at work until you can get the ideas across without skipping a beat.

In addition to this short description, you will also need to be prepared for a longer and more detailed explanation of HPT.

Selling HPT as a Concept and a Practice

Training organizations are often in the position of selling courses, or a new approach to course delivery (such as satellite or web delivery), or the need to conduct an assessment before defining a curriculum. Selling management and your internal or external clients on HPT may seem like a different and difficult process. Your clients may not have any idea what HPT is and they may have trouble imagining how it can help them. Both formal and informal opportunities for the use of an expanded definition, description, and vision of HPT will occur.

You need to have a compelling presentation you can show to everyone who will listen. This presentation should introduce the concept and the benefits of HPT. It should make it obvious that pursuing a data-driven approach to performance issues will increase the success of your company. Give your presentation at department meetings, on career days, and anywhere you can collect an audience. Build awareness at every level of the organization and people will begin to sell HPT for you.

Use the following presentation elements, which are all described in more detail in the following paragraphs, to build your own presentation in your own words:

- Introduction
- What's a problem?
- A graphic of the human performance system
- A definition of HPT
- Examples of situations where training was the wrong answer
- Assumptions about classroom training
- Your model for HPT
- What's different about HPT?
- Conclusion
- Anticipating objections

Introduction

As in any good presentation, be sure to include something that will spark and attract the attention of your audience. Introduce yourself, make sure that any other appropriate introductions are handled, and begin to build rapport with your audience. Let people know what you hope to accomplish with this presentation, and provide a short organizer—for example, a list of your three main points.

Then you can move into the body of your presentation, which will describe your main points, provide supporting evidence for them, examine possible objections, and show how HPT will provide benefits that far outweigh any objections.

What's a Problem?

This section of your presentation focuses on how HPT identifies customer needs. For example, customers seldom *need* a training program (or a reorganization or a team-building exercise). What they *really want* is a solution to some problem. *Problems* generally result in a loss of time or resources or money.

Bob Mager, in *What Every Manager Should Know About Training* (1992), provides a wonderful and humorous way to characterize problems. Actually it is more of a way to characterize what problems are *not*. The list includes the statement "I have an aspirin problem." If the person has a headache, for example, aspirin may be the solution. The headache is the problem. But what is causing the headache? If the headache is due to excessive noise in the environment or to a lack of nourishment, aspirin will not provide a long-term solution. Earplugs, noise abatement, or a good lunch may be more likely to solve the problem. Taking aspirin might mask the problem for a while, but it will come back without a more root cause solution.

"I have an aspirin problem" is much the same construction as "I have a training problem." People do not actually have "training problems" unless there is something wrong with their training. What they may have are problems that are related to a lack of knowledge or skill in their employees. But if those problems are really related to something else, for example, motivational or environmental causes, then training alone will not solve them.

During your presentation you need to communicate the message that training is not the answer to every business problem. It is often the first idea that managers have about how to solve things that go wrong, or how to introduce something new. You need to find a catchy, attention-getting way to make it clear that people have *business problems*, not *training problems*, and that identifying what the problem really is before prescribing a solution is essential to solving it.

A Graphic of the Human Performance System

The human performance system provides a wonderful way to look at the systemic nature of problems. What is the human performance system at your company? The human performance system we use at Redwood Mountain Counsulting is presented in Figure 2.1.

When you present this graphic, you want to make it clear that there are a host of potential root causes of business problems. Business issues occur within a system. Make it clear to your audience that if you address only part of a system or always try to provide one kind of solution, many of the potential causes of problems may not be addressed. Also make the point that there can be a number of root causes to a problem. All serious causes should be addressed or the problem will most likely not be solved.

A Definition of HPT

Define HPT in simple and plain language. By now you should have already created such a definition that works for you and your department. For example, "Performance technology is a step-by-step method for quickly defining a business problem, figuring out what causes it, and then removing the barriers to achieving the desired business results."

Examples of Situations Where Training Was the Wrong Answer

Choose three simple, relevant examples of requests for training. To make your presentation go quickly and smoothly, these simple examples should have easy-to-grasp root causes. For example, skills training was requested but the main issue was some environmental barrier. Or knowledge training was requested but the real issue was motivation: perhaps employees did not achieve the required performance because they did not see the value of it, or perhaps they believed that what they were being asked to do was either too hard or too easy. Your third example should be a training request where a lack of skills or knowledge really *was* the problem. If there was some other aspect of this third example that required another kind of intervention in addition to training, so much the better. For example, people didn't know how to do something (training turned out to be a right answer) and, in addition, the policy they should follow was not clear (the policy had to be clarified). Stress the point that multiple interventions, or solution sets, are often needed to ensure that the significant barriers to performance are eliminated.

Assumptions About Classroom Training

Include a message in your presentation that classroom training can be a wonderful thing, but also emphasize that such training is too often based on unwarranted assumptions. These mistaken assumptions include:

- *Everyone starts with the same knowledge.* This is almost never true.
- *Everyone learns at the same pace.* This is almost never true.
- *Everyone learns best from listening.* The single most important factor influencing learning is, in fact, practice.
- *Everyone will bridge naturally from theory to application.* This is seldom true. The ability to recite or even explain a theory is a far cry from the ability to actually apply that theory.
- *Everyone should learn individually rather than collaboratively.* Of course people do learn individually, whether they are doing solo or group activities in class. But are the objectives and activities of the training tailored to learning in such a way that the participants

learn how to perform in collaboration with others? Usually collaboration is necessary in a work setting.

- *Learning is the transfer of knowledge from a teacher to a passive learner.* Many classes are run as if this were the case. Actually, before learning takes place, learners must actively connect what they are learning with what they already know. Without individual processing, the teacher is just pouring knowledge into a porous vessel.

Does this mean that training is on its way out? Often by this point in your presentation some people in your audience get the impression that you are calling for the end to all forms of training. Of course you are not saying that. There will always be many things that people need to learn, so there will always be a need for training. But the focus of training or any other intervention should be on the ability of the participant or employee to meet performance goals. And you want to be sure that when training is the right solution, or part of the right solution, it will meet those goals.

Your Model for HPT

You should show your model for HPT. It should be simple enough for people to understand the essence of it with just a little explanation. You should have a model that you and members of your department agree makes sense for your organization.

What's Different About HPT?

With HPT the focus is always on performance, on the ability to get results. Some training departments focus on behavior: "Let's instill this or that behavior in our participants and that will be a good thing for the organization." But knowledge, skills, behaviors, and attitudes are means to performance, not ends in themselves. Training that does not affect on-the-job performance does not make a contribution and is therefore a wasted investment. With HPT the focus is on results: "Let's ensure that we have removed the barriers that are getting in the way of achieving our desired business results."

Rather than assuming that many business problems can be solved by providing more training courses, your company will begin to address problems systemically as a matter of course. Managers and performance improvement professionals from various disciplines will look for the root cause of problems rather than simply attending to the symptoms presented by the problem. They will also be sure to plan for the "domino effect" that making a change in one part of the system may have on another part of the system.

The results of these changes in thinking and action will enable your company to develop a serious competitive advantage over companies that do not make this change. When carried out well, not only will the individual HPT projects save your company time and money, but they will also encourage all who see them to begin to think and act differently when confronted with business and performance issues. This change in thinking and action will have positive consequences that flow directly to the bottom line.

Conclusion

As you should do when you conclude any presentation, briefly review your main points. Add to the persuasiveness of your presentation by providing a brief visualization of the benefits of HPT. To close your presentation with impact, you may wish to ask for a follow-up action from your audience. Leave plenty of time for questions. You should be ready to field questions that may include doubts about HPT.

Anticipating Objections

Of course, you will want to prepare ahead of time for the objections managers and others may raise regarding the implementation of HPT at your company. After you've talked with a number of people about HPT, you may begin to see a pattern. Objections may be related to a variety of factors, including charters, expertise, "flavor of the month" fears, the status quo, and the like.

Charter

The charter issue may involve other performance improvement organizations within your company. Often, the human resources department may see their domain as overlapping that of HPT. So, too, may the organizational development folks, if you have them. Other companies may feel that their own managers are expected to look at things systemically and that they therefore have no need of your help in this area. The truth is that HPT grew out of the field of instructional design. And it continues to have a close relationship with it. Many training departments have struggled with what to do when training does not solve their customers' problems; some of them have adapted an HPT approach without realizing that this is the name for what they do. And other organizations often find it compelling, too. It actually makes sense for all these groups to practice at least an HPT mind-set, that is, to approach all performance issues with these questions in mind: What's the problem? What causes it? What solutions will give us the results we want?

Some companies may wish to have performance analysts who are chartered to analyze problems or opportunities and then to recommend solutions. Depending on which solutions are recommended, a team of people from training, human resources, organizational development, compensation, information technology, human factors, or other areas may be employed to create the solutions. Other companies have combined many of their once separate performance improvement organizations into one larger organization and then left them alone to work out internally who is best suited to work on which projects. Still other companies have decided to teach the HPT approach to everyone who could reasonably use it so that a systemic and systematic approach becomes characteristic of the way their people work.

Expertise

If people are in the habit of thinking of your training department as one that just responds reactively to training requests, they may have trouble picturing course developers and training facilitators as ready and able to solve their business problems. It helps to emphasize that HPT is the practice of solving human performance problems that are getting in the way of achieving business results. Management defines the results they want. The performance consultant investigates what knowledge, motivation, or environmental barriers may be in the way of getting those business results.

Performance consultants must have more than a passing idea of what the company does, how it runs, and what factors generate revenue. For example, if your training specialist has been in manufacturing training for five years and cannot tell you in general how parts arrive at the company, how these parts are assembled into products, and how the final products are shipped to customers, then you should not assign this person to help a manufacturing manager solve her business problems. Performance consultants need to do their homework about an organization so that they can credibly help it to resolve business issues. The good news is that a performance consultant gets to ask a lot of questions. So it is possible for someone to walk into a new organization and to learn what is necessary to help that organization meet its goals by asking the right questions. But if that person has been in that organization for a long time, make sure he or she knows enough to be credible before interacting with the customers.

Flavor of the Month

Some managers have been involved in so many different management or improvement approaches that they really do not want to hear about yet one more. They may have invested time and resources in figuring out how to follow some other methodology only to have it fade as a passing fad. This kind of experience often leads to cynicism. We have heard of at least one senior manager at a well-known Fortune 100 company who has told the various departments vying for work in supporting his department that he does not want to see another model or hear any more jargon. He simply wants someone to tell him, in plain language, how his problem will be solved.

You can do this. Approach your opportunities to talk about HPT as opportunities to talk about solving problems related to people's performance. First you're going to figure out what the problem is, next you're going to figure out what causes the problem, and then you're going to provide solutions. Easy. And you can talk about training. They're familiar with training. So you say, "We're going to see if this is a problem that training can solve. If it is, great. If not, then we'll recommend something else. Or, it may be that something in the environment needs to change to make sure that the training will work. If so, we'd like to be sure to include that in our recommendations."

Status Quo

Sometimes other training managers will be most reluctant to hear anything about HPT. They are used to thinking of themselves as training managers or as training professionals. Sometimes they are so successful at what they are doing now that they may view changing approaches as an unnecessary personal risk. Or their funding model may require them to generate revenue from charging course fees; if they offer less training, they will have fewer dollars. This may even cause them to miss their financial goals. If the system at your company is such that it will not support the practice of HPT, then you may need to gather quietly some success stories and then pitch making some gradual (or more radical) changes in the system.

There may be other objections to HPT at your company, objections we haven't touched on here. As you discover what they are, develop a response that

1. Is respectful of the person raising the objection

2. Acknowledges the truth that is probably inherent in at least part of the objection

3. Provides additional information and a vision about how HPT can serve your company

Following this advice should help you to meet and overcome any objection.

As you talk with individuals and give presentations to groups you will encounter objections such as those listed here. It will also be wise for you to anticipate the change management and political issues that will necessarily be connected to making the transition to HPT.

Change Management and Political Issues

Making a shift in focus as big as moving from training to HPT requires attention to change management and to the politics of getting work done in your company. Even if many people are excited about the possibilities associated with this big change, others will meet it with uncertainty or even resistance. This will be true of the training and development staff as well as of your management and your customers. Just as you would do in any other intervention, you need to be prepared to help manage the changes inherent in this transition process.

At first, when people are becoming aware of the change, you will need to provide an introduction to HPT. Tell people about it briefly and emphasize its benefits.

As people become more curious, they will want more information. They may start to express concerns about how HPT will change things. They'll be asking questions such as

"What is happening?"

"What will be different?"

"How will my job change?"

"What will happen to the interpersonal relationships I have now with my colleagues and customers?"

"Will I be able to learn enough about HPT to either do it or to contract for it?"

They will require enough information to begin to visualize how work will be different with HPT. This is when they will need to hear success stories. If you can provide your fellow employees, management, and customers with testimonials from others who have benefited from HPT, this would be a plus.

Your change may be made gradually. If that is the case, then one or two early adopters may serve first as pioneers in HPT and then as role models for those who make the change later on. And you can provide training, tools, mentoring, job aids, and other support for training professionals who don't know how to do HPT. For managers who may use this new service, a great strategy is to give them some information about how to engage with performance technologists. You can do that with meetings, or presentations, or by giving them a copy of Mager's *What Every Manager Should Know About Training* (1992).

As time goes on and HPT becomes part of the way people do business at your company, you will want to ensure that continued support and recognition is available for your new performance technologists.

Working with Politics

A fact of life in most companies is that reengineering any function is likely to incite political reactions in the form of turf wars, power struggles, people digging in their heels, and more. Be prepared, don't be surprised, and don't take it personally. Some people may behave in surprising ways. If you find that you are unsure of someone's motives for resisting or even fighting the implementation of HPT, "follow the money."

It is often true that training managers are rewarded for the number of courses in their catalog, the number of students they put through classes, and the revenue they generate (even if in the form of internal transfer dollars). Consider the training manager's point of view: Why, when they are rewarded for offering courses and they've figured out how to do it well, would they want to change to HPT? In fact, if a training manager successfully dissuades an organization from putting one hundred people through a training class they don't need, she may risk not making her financial goals. Sometimes the environmental barriers to implementing HPT make it difficult for training departments to recommend and implement any solutions other than training.

This means that you may have to take a bit of your own medicine. Figure out what the barriers are to having your training department switch to HPT. In other words, you may have to do a performance analysis on implementing HPT in your organization. Define the business results the company needs, figure out what barriers are in the way, and recommend solutions to remove those barriers. It may take a bit of creative accounting. Detailed suggestions for doing this are available in Chapter Seven.

Managers generally love the idea of HPT. It may be the first time they've seen a performance improvement approach that includes business measures. They are generally easy to convince. If you convince managers first, your other training and human resource professionals may find that it will be politically difficult to resist moving in an HPT direction. But be prepared to point out that some structural changes may be required, either in finance models, goal setting, or reward systems before a successful HPT program can be sustained.

Summary

In this chapter we have focused on various communications you will need to prepare for as you help your organization become aware of HPT. Making sure that those who will practice HPT can articulate the concept and its benefits and finding ways to present information about HPT to your potential customers are keys to successful implementation. Here are some of the main points from this chapter:

- Explaining HPT in plain language works best, but doing it well takes practice.

- You'll have to sell HPT as a concept and a practice. This will require time and effort.

- HPT will change the way people work and how they think about work. Be able to describe those changes and why they are of benefit.

- Create a compelling presentation and deliver it to any-one who will listen.

- Training is not going away, but you can make sure that the training you do offer is the right training.

- Your job is not to provide training; your job is to solve performance problems to achieve business results.

- You will have to manage change and political processes to make the transition to HPT.

In the next chapter we take a more detailed look at how to identify and address organizational barriers to HPT. Experiencing resistance is one thing, figuring out what causes the resistance and how to overcome it is another. We show you how to use the HPT model to fix barriers to HPT. This will also provide an opportunity for practice.

7

Analyzing and Addressing Organizational Barriers to HPT

Smooth sailing into an easy implementation of HPT would be a delight. Unfortunately, you may have to deal with shoals, sandbars, reefs, and other navigational hazards before you reach port. In this chapter, we discuss finding and addressing potential barriers to HPT in your company. Using an HPT approach to analyze a company's barriers to instituting HPT is a great way to practice the HPT methodology.

We walk you through a process of analyzing and providing solutions for overcoming organizational barriers to implementing HPT. To do this, we follow our HPT model. (See Chapter Two for a more detailed description of the model.) The process is presented in this chapter within the following sections:

Problem Definition

Identifying and Validating Suspected Gaps and Barriers to HPT

Suggested Remedies for Common Barriers to Implementing HPT

Implementing Solutions to HPT Barriers

Problem Definition

First, start with your general vision of what HPT will do for your company. This "problem definition" might be thought of as really more of an "opportunity description." It may read something like this:

> By implementing HPT, XYZ Productions will address performance problems in a systemic and systematic way, thereby eliminating barriers that are keeping us from achieving our business goals. HPT has the potential to improve performance by 10 to 1 or greater over less systemic approaches, and therefore can assist XYZ Productions in maintaining its competitive advantage in our industry.

You will want to have some way to measure whether your HPT implementation has been a useful addition to your company. This will make it clear to management that you have sound reasons for your goal of implementing HPT. You must say something more inspiring to management than "I want to add HPT because other companies are doing it." You will want to have a more tangible performance goal, one related to saving time, money, or effort.

The sample problem definition above mentions "10 to 1" performance gains. This goal may sound overly optimistic. But many HPT practitioners are reporting gains exceeding 10 to 1. Indeed, they also report feeling some trepidation about pointing to such high figures because they believe that it will be difficult for people to accept them as true. Take our word for it, 10 to 1 sounds great and is actually a conservative estimate of HPT success. If you use this ratio, it will sound impressive and compelling to your listeners. Moreover, given the potential for improvement existing in many companies, a 10 to 1 improvement may be relatively easy to achieve.

Next, determine what you would accept as evidence that HPT is adding a substantial benefit to your company. For example, you may state that with HPT performance gains will be measured for the first time in terms of solving business results. You may want to commit yourself to the 10 to 1 ratio. You may also decide to compare the cost of providing what was requested (such as training) with what was eventually delivered (which may or may not have included training) to determine what savings were eventually gained by the HPT intervention. See more about how to measure the results of your interventions in Chapter Five.

You have just completed the first two steps of the problem definition phase of the HPT model. Now you will want to validate your efforts with your staff, your manager, and anyone else who should have a stake in your progress to this point. Make sure that the appropriate stakeholders have no major disagreements and that you have not left out anything important in your statement of the issue and your definition of desired outcomes. It is critical to obtain buy-in at this stage, and to maintain the support of appropriate people in your organization throughout the whole process. Figure 7.1 highlights where we are now in the HPT model.

Identifying and Validating Suspected Gaps and Barriers to HPT

When you are implementing a new system and trying to figure out where the difficulties might be, you should create a list of potential barriers to full and successful implementation. Then, as you roll out your implementation, you can use this list in a dynamic fashion to check what *actually happens* against what you *anticipated might happen*. After all, things will probably change as you go along. In other words, no matter how carefully you have tried to anticipate issues, some will probably occur that you did not expect. Frequent monitoring of potential problems can help you to recognize problem issues that do occur early in their development, when they are easiest to handle.

When you look at your organization, use the human performance system (Figure 2.1) as a framework to identify potential barriers to implementing HPT. Using the elements in the system, compare what you believe will assist versus what you think will hinder your company in implementing HPT. Here are the steps to follow:

Figure 7.1. The First Part of Problem Definition.

Start with the business issue and figure out what outcomes you are aiming for.

Problem Definition			
Identify business issue	Define desired outcomes	Analyze current system	Identify gaps

1. *Identify positive and negative forces for HPT for each subelement in the human performance system.* The negative forces are anticipated gaps in your system that you may need to address before HPT can be fully realized. For example, managers at your company may do an excellent job of making their business goals clear, which would be a positive factor in the organizational goals of the human performance system. Negative forces are anticipated gaps in your system that you may need to address before HPT can be fully realized. To make these identifications, you can employ a number of techniques, such as conducting interviews or holding focus groups.

2. *Speculate about what is causing or will cause these gaps.* You are trying to identify root causes. Each root cause will be due to a problem related to (a) knowledge and skills, (b) motivation, and/or (c) the environment. Identify which of these three areas (or combination of areas) you believe the barrier to performance stems from and provide some detail about the nature of the barrier. For example, with a knowledge and skills problem, it may be that the employees do not know how to follow a particular procedure. Or they may not have had enough practice to perform the procedure fluently. With a motivation problem, people may not realize why they should invest effort in the required activity, or they may be overconfident or underconfident about their ability to perform that activity. Environmental barriers include causal factors that do not reside inside the individual, for example, the physical surroundings, the availability of tools and information, processes that are

confusing, hierarchical management structures that encourage difficulties, and so on.

3. *Figure out how you will validate whether the root causes you suspect to be the source of gaps are the actual causes of gaps.* One's initial speculations about the true root causes of a problem can be deceiving. For example, an apparent knowledge and skills problem may actually turn out to be a motivational issue or an environmental issue. The best way to avoid errors in pinpointing root causes is to observe what people are actually doing and/or to interview them to determine what is really happening. While you are observing or interviewing, you will need to keep three key questions in mind: (a) Do they know how to do it? (b) Have they chosen not to do it, or do they have an unrealistic estimation of their abilities (either too high or too low) that keeps them from investing the right amount of effort? and (c) What environmental factor is missing or getting in their way that keeps them from doing the desired performance? Figure 7.2 highlights the sections of the HPT model that you are about to tackle.

Figure 7.2. Finishing Problem Definition and Planning to Validate Root Causes.

Use the Human Performance System as a framework for analyzing the current system and identifying current and possible gaps. Make your best guess about what type of barriers are causing those gaps, and then plan to validate whether you were correct.

Problem Definition			
Identify business issue	Define desired outcomes	Analyze current system	Identify gaps

Root Cause Analysis			
Identify knowledge barriers	Identify motivation barriers	Identify environmental barriers	Validate causes

We designed the following "thumbnail sketches" to provide examples of both positive and negative forces that have an impact on the implementation of HPT in a sample company, Blue Star Enterprises (BSE). In these sketches, we detail the suspected root causes of identified gaps and provide notes about how to validate those barriers. Your company will be different, of course, but you can use the BSE case as a model for your own investigation.

Sample Thumbnail Sketch: Organizational Inputs

After examining Blue Star Enterprises's stated and implicit goals, values, and climate, we found both positive and negative forces for HPT. We have speculated about what may be causing the gaps in performance and provided a plan for validating those causes.

Organization Goals

We looked at whether HPT was in alignment with BSE's goals. Organizational goals are long-term and short-term objectives that have been adopted by a company, business unit, department, or team.

Positive force for HPT. BSE has a keen desire to solve business problems. Management believes this is necessary to remain competitive and in business. As one executive noted to us, "If we're not on top of problems, the competition will eat our lunch."

Negative force for HPT (gap). Managers note that sometimes BSE is in such a rush to achieve its quarterly results that the underlying system is never fully considered when a business problem comes up. This can result in short-term solutions that do not address the root causes of performance gaps.

Suspected barrier. This gap may be a motivation problem related to choice and effort. If managers generally understood the possibility, importance, and utility of addressing the root causes of problems, they might choose to do so and insist that those who work under their direction invest the required effort to provide more robust solutions.

Plan to validate. Using some examples of recent problems that were given a short-term but not systemic solution, we can check with a few managers to find out whether they believed that a more robust solution was possible.

Organization Values

For BSE's values as they support HPT, we examined what management stated was important to them and also which behaviors or results were rewarded. We looked for connections between what was valued and the behaviors and results expected from the practice of HPT.

Positive force for HPT. BSE highly values being first to market, best in class, and maximizing employee contributions.

Negative force for HPT (gap). BSE overvalues employee contributions toward achieving short-term results, and consequently undervalues long-term employee development and strategic planning.

Suspected barrier. This may be an environmental issue related to consequences. Although the most senior managers seem to value the long-term view, and although they sometimes exhort their subordinates to value a longer view (in balance with the short-term realities), BSE's rewards, incentives, and recognition programs center on short-term results.

Plan to validate. Check the existing rewards, incentives, and recognition programs to ensure that they are in fact designed to encourage a focus on short-term results. Also check with a sample of managers and employees to see if their perceptions of what is rewarded match actual practice. In other words, do they believe that short-term rather than long-term results and solutions will be rewarded?

Organization Climate

Looking at the climate of the corporation and HPT, we were concerned with the feeling tones of the culture. For example, what was the sense of urgency and how "political" does one have to be to succeed?

Positive force for HPT. Strong forces in the BSE climate include paying attention to business and business results, staying focused on the problem at hand, and promoting an egalitarian culture.

Negative force for HPT (gap). There is a hurry-up quality to the BSE culture that makes it difficult for those (managers and employees alike) who want to expend effort on strategic projects. There is a company-wide mentality that says, "What have you done for me lately?"

Suspected barrier. This gap may be an environmental problem related to information gaps and a skewed rewards system. Employees and managers may not have internalized the fact that senior management wants to move toward a more strategic way of doing business and solving problems. Moreover, the reward systems are not aligned to reward longer term, strategic results.

Plan to validate. Using some short case studies that clearly illustrate tactical and strategic projects as our tools, we will ask managers to rate which projects they believe would be most important to management at BSE. We will also ask them to suggest the most likely rewards for successfully finishing each project.

Job Standards and Expectations

We checked to see whether clear standards and expectations were in place for each job at BSE. When managers and employees have a mutual understanding of what should be accomplished, that is a positive force for the achievement of business goals.

Positive force for HPT. Job standards at BSE are clear, up-to-date, and well communicated, which means that managers and employees have readily available information about what is expected for each job.

Negative force for HPT (gap). None.

Suspected barrier. N/A.

Plan to validate. N/A

Sample Thumbnail Sketch: People

The knowledge, skill, and attitudes possessed by the people in an organization make a significant impact on whether HPT will find a congenial home there. We looked for experience and education that would be compatible with an HPT approach.

Positive force for HPT. A few people inside BSE's training department actually have some background in and experience with HPT. Those without experience are receptive to the idea of implementing HPT and are eager to learn how to do it. In addition, a number of people in other departments have related skills in systematic approaches to problem solving. For example, some of the organizational development folks use a related process. The quality department uses a systematic process. Engineers, in general, have studied and used systems theory to diagnose and solve problems.

Negative force for HPT (gap). A general lack of knowledge at BSE about the positive benefits of a systems approach to human performance could be a major problem. Also, many people at BSE who could be employing HPT, either at a basic mind-set level or as full-blown HPT consultants, just do not know how to do so.

Suspected barrier. There is a widespread lack of knowledge and skills directly related to HPT at BSE.

Plan to validate. We will perform a needs analysis to (1) determine what similar knowledge and skills exist and (2) determine exactly where the gap in knowledge and skills is.

Sample Thumbnail Sketch: Behaviors

Behaviors that people employ in their work may or may not contribute to the accomplishment of desired business results. Behaviors include the thoughts, actions, decisions, and problem-solving activities that managers and employees use in their work.

Positive force for HPT. The intellectual capabilities of BSE people tend to be well developed, so their ability to solve problems and make decisions is strong. Their confidence is high, so they readily engage in problem-solving and decision-making tasks.

Negative force for HPT (gap). When problems arise at BSE, there is a tendency to treat symptoms instead of the root causes of those problems. Decisions are often made quickly, before all the important facts are gathered. Later, initial decisions may be reversed, but by then efforts made to implement the first decision are well under way. This causes rework, lost time and missed opportunities, and a certain amount of frustration.

Suspected barrier. BSE suffers from a lack of knowledge and skill in applying a systemic and systematic approach to decision making and problem solving. (See also the suspected barriers related to organizational inputs.)

Plan to validate. We will investigate, using an interview process, the processes used in problem solving and decision making in both performance improvement and line organizations at BSE. We will carefully examine one or two recent decisions or problem solutions to determine whether the people involved used or knew how to use a systemic and/or systematic approach.

Sample Thumbnail Sketch: Performance

An awareness of and attention to the actual results of job-related behaviors will make a tremendous difference in whether or not HPT is likely to be embraced in an organization. We looked at the current performance solutions being employed by the organization and whether they were perceived to be achieving the desired results.

Positive force for HPT. There have been some recent high-profile projects at BSE where managerial assumptions about what training could accomplish and the actual results of implementing that training clearly did not match. Although negative results in themselves, these training failures have caused BSE managers to reexamine their assumptions about the value of training itself, which is a positive step toward changing the current system. Many of these managers are open to trying new approaches, and this openness can be harnessed to implement HPT.

Negative force for HPT (gap). Performance consulting is not being done at BSE today. Currently problems are being solved and decisions are being made without a performance analysis model to determine the systemic root causes of problems or to figure out how a new opportunity will affect the entire system.

Suspected barrier. BSE suffers from a lack of knowledge and skill about how to conduct a performance analysis and how to remove barriers to performance by means other than training in the organization. BSE also has environmental barriers in the form of a lack of process, information, and tools for performance consulting.

Plan to validate. Because HPT is a new process for almost everyone who might be involved with it at BSE, these barriers are self-evident.

Sample Thumbnail Sketch: Consequences

Consequences include such things as rewards, incentives, recognition, status, and increased responsibilities. They can be positive or negative.

Positive force for HPT. Once BSE decides to take on a business process, managers are pretty consistent about putting positive consequences in place for people who learn and execute the process well.

Negative force for HPT (gap). A possible negative force once HPT is championed at BSE could be a confusion over consequences for this new process and outcomes versus already-existing consequences for training managers and individual contributors.

Suspected barrier. If this becomes a problem, then it will most likely be due to an environmental barrier—that of confused processes.

Plan to validate. We need to monitor the impressions of managers and employees regarding the new consequences associated with HPT implementation. We will look for conflicting rewards and for confusion about what is expected.

Sample Thumbnail Sketch: Feedback

Feedback about performance, consequences, or any other element of the human performance system can be transmitted to individual people, to groups of people, to an organization as a whole, to a specific job category, and so on.

Positive force for HPT. Feedback mechanisms in common use at BSE include regular one-on-one meetings between managers and employees, regular weekly or biweekly staff meetings, quarterly department meetings, widely read electronic newsletters, and various reviews for individuals and organizations. Thus the system for delivering feedback is multifaceted and strong.

Negative force for HPT (gap). Possible issues with feedback at BSE might include conflicting messages if the consequences of implementing HPT are confusing or not consistent with encouraging the adoption of HPT. Feedback messages could well be delivered ineffectively if those giving the feedback do not understand what performance to look for (that is, performance that would indicate a successful implementation of HPT).

Suspected barrier. Because the feedback mechanisms at BSE are currently working well, issues with feedback would stem from errors in the environment. That is, if the consequences are not assigned appropriately, then the feedback will reflect those errors.

Plan to validate. We will use the same procedure as with consequences, should they become a barrier.

Sample Thumbnail Sketch: Environment

We looked at environmental helps and hindrances to implementing HPT at BSE. Environmental factors include processes, information, and tools. A company that resists creating processes, that creates irrational processes, or that fails to provide sufficient information or tools for performance may prove to have significant barriers to implementing HPT.

Positive force for HPT. BSE has efficient mechanisms for transmitting processes, information, and tools to managers and employees.

Negative force for HPT (gap). BSE does not currently have any processes or tools to assist with implementing HPT.

Suspected barrier. BSE has no goals to create processes and tools specific to implementation of HPT. This is possibly a motivation issue; management underconfidence may be discouraging engagement in creating processes and tools for HPT at BSE. The company suffers from a current lack of wide-ranging support for developing processes and tools (an environmental issue).

Plan to validate. We need to start with those who have some knowledge of and experience with HPT. We need to check to see if there are any resources available to provide guidelines for processes and tools for those who are new to the field. We should check on the motivation issue at the same time: What do the people at BSE believe would be necessary to create the required processes and tools? Do they believe they can be successful in creating them? Why or why not? Because HPT is new at BSE, there are not-yet-stated goals in place to support the creation of processes, information, and tools.

You may find that the barriers related in the Blue Star Enterprises case are similar to ones that you discover in your organization. Now, let's move on to looking at ways to overcome these barriers.

Solution Implementation

As we suggested earlier, barriers to HPT will come in three major areas: knowledge and skills, motivation, and the environment. Once you know in which areas your barriers fall, you can gauge with confidence what solutions to put in place to eliminate them. As highlighted in Figure 7.3, you are selecting a solution set to eliminate performance barriers. Now you are beginning the last phase of the HPT model: solution implementation.

Barriers related to a lack of knowledge and skills require some form of learning to occur. Solutions often include training of one kind or another, either leader-led or self-instructional. It is also possible to eliminate these barriers with self-directed learning in which the learner creates an individualized program of study from information and goals found in books, on the Web, from colleagues, and by using other resources. This may or may not be the right answer for you and your organization, depending on the sophistication of your learners' self-directed learning skills. (We provide more information on the development of individual knowledge and skills in Chapter Nine.)

Solutions for a lack of motivation can be addressed by assisting with two major processes: choice and effort (see Clark, 1988). When presented with a particular choice about something to do, does the individual have sufficient interest in, attach enough importance to,

Figure 7.3. Selecting the Solution Set.

Once you have identified the barriers to implementing HPT in your organization, then you can select the solutions that will eliminate those barriers.

Solution Implementation			
Select solution set	Design interventions	Develop interventions	Implement solutions

or perceive enough usefulness in that particular thing to choose to do it? If not, can that individual be encouraged to see how interesting or important or useful it is? Even once something is chosen, a person may decline to work hard enough to succeed at it. In that case, he may feel either that the task is too easy for him to bother working at it with much diligence or, conversely, that the task is too difficult for him to even bother trying. In both cases, assuming that the individual in question is the right person to accomplish the task, the prescription is the same: he needs to invest more effort. The person who thinks that a particular task is too easy is overconfident. When people are overconfident, they need to be convinced that the activity or task in question is more demanding than they think and that they need to invest more effort to succeed. The person who thinks that a particular task is too hard is underconfident. One good way to deal with underconfidence is to divide a task or project into smaller, more obviously "doable" segments. As individuals master each small segment in the process, they will gradually develop confidence that they can accomplish the larger task (and become more motivated to do so).

Environmental barriers involve problems with information, processes, or tools. They involve things like irrational processes or unknown goals. Unlike motivational issues or a lack of knowledge and skills, environmental barriers exist outside individual employees or managers. Removing environmental barriers involves solutions like manipulating physical surroundings, making more information or better tools available, or creating or modifying processes.

Suggested Remedies

Once you have determined and validated which barriers apply to your organization, you will have to figure out what to do about them. The following lists explain some common barriers and provide some useful solutions to them. You should find that reviewing these barriers and solutions helps you in your own diagnostic process.

First we list barriers related to knowledge and skills.

• *People don't know how to do HPT.* When HPT is new to an organization, those who will be expected to practice it may not know how. It will be important to create development plans for those who need to learn HPT. See Chapter Nine for more information about how to create development plans.

• *People don't know how to create solutions other than training.* The first thing to do when confronted with this issue is to relax. Nobody knows how to develop all the possible solutions that can be employed to help improve human performance: there are just too many of them! Many HPT practitioners become experts at the disciplines required for one or more types of solutions, such as instructional design or organizational development. Then, in time and with practice, they learn to design other types of solutions. More important, they learn how to recognize when a particular situation calls for a particular type of solution. They develop a network of colleagues who specialize in providing a wide variety of interventions. Then, when the solution calls for an intervention outside their own areas of expertise, they know where to turn for help. Here are some things you can do to increase your department's ability to respond to requirements for solutions other than training:

1. Identify the types of interventions you expect to employ most often.

2. Determine if there is someone on your staff who can provide each type of intervention on your list.

3. For those items on your list that are new to everyone on your staff, see if you can identify others in your company who could be called in to help with those interventions. For example, someone in HR may be able to help with designing reward systems or someone in information systems may be able to help with designing an e-mail distribution system that will provide information to people more efficiently.

4. Where you still have gaps in terms of intervention types, delegate someone in your department to find an external resource to fill the gap, or assign someone the task of learning how to perform this type of intervention him- or herself.

5. Ask different members of your staff to investigate different probable or possible interventions that could be required. Assign each to give a twenty-minute presentation about what they have learned about that intervention at your staff meetings. Ask them to be sure to include information about what kinds of problems the intervention will solve and how to tell when this intervention will be the right answer. Alternatively, ask experts to provide the presentations instead.

• *Managers don't know when to request HPT services.* As you introduce HPT into the broader organization, managers will hear you and others talk about how it can help to solve business problems. Such word of mouth will raise consciousness about HPT and help the implementation process. Here are some other things you can do to increase managers' awareness of HPT:

1. Photocopy interesting articles about HPT success stories or on the HPT approach in general and distribute them either generally or to targeted managers when the timing seems right.

2. Suggest an HPT approach when it is appropriate. Once the project is off to a successful start, for example, or once it is concluded, you can let the manager know when to consider asking for HPT in the future.

3. If you have influence over management training and development efforts at your company, include a section on "When to Ask for HPT" in the appropriate course.

4. Include HPT success stories in best practices reports or databases in your company's knowledge management system.

• *Managers don't know how to support the implementation of HPT.* Once you have convinced upper management or even a single manager that HPT will provide an improvement in business results, you may want to help them to become HPT champions. This may require some diplomatic coaching on your part. The following strategies may help you:

1. Provide them with a checklist of helpful actions they can take.

2. Hold regular status meetings in which you report on the progress you have made in implementing HPT and let them know how they can help.

3. If you are working with a number of managers in different organizations, you may wish to assign a member of your staff to work as an HPT liaison with managers in each of those organizations. Your liaisons can then uncover issues, make suggestions, and provide coaching as appropriate.

• *Managers don't know how to provide consequences or feedback for HPT efforts.* You may have to help your own management to see how to reward your department differently. For example, you may be currently measured in terms of the number of courses in your catalog, the number of students who take classes, or the ratings students give your courses. Such measures of success will not be improved by your HPT efforts. In fact, if you offer fewer classes as a result of finding other ways to improve performance, measures such as courses offered or students attending courses may drop dramatically. If you continue to be judged by old measures, your success in implementing HPT would actually harm you and your department. This would certainly discourage you from implementing HPT. Explore with your manager how your goals, consequences, and feedback may need to be redesigned to support you in implementing HPT.

Now we turn our attention to barriers related to motivation.

• *Nobody recognizes what HPT could do for this organization.* Executives, managers, HR, training, and other performance improvement professionals will not support HPT if they do not understand why they should even be interested in it. You will need to make sure that people see the value and importance of attacking business problems and opportunities by using HPT. Success stories, either internal or external, should help. Make sure you collect such stories, complete with metrics showing a significant saving of time, money, or resources because of using an HPT process, and share them with the organization.

• *There is no value here for strategic, holistic, or systematic thinking.* If everything is done at your company with an eye for tactics rather than strategy, or for fire fighting (merely treating a problem) rather than for fire prevention (finding the root cause of the problem), you're facing a difficult motivational hurdle. To obtain permission to begin a performance analysis, you will have to choose your words carefully.

Do not talk about *strategy, systems thinking,* or *systematic processes.* Instead, suggest that you may have a way to solve the problem that will save time and money. If a manager is asking for a training program on X and you believe (because you have some knowledge of the problem already) that a quicker, cheaper, and/or better solution is available, create a one-page recommendation that outlines your proposed solution. Use simple language and emphasize the efficiency of your solution.

- *Some people think they are already doing HPT but they're not.* HPT requires a fair amount of knowledge, skill, effort, and practice to do well. Some people believe that if they are creating any performance intervention that is not training—for example, job aids—that they are practicing HPT. HPT, of course, is not defined by the type of solution used to solve a problem but rather by the systematic process used to solve the root causes of business problems related to human performance.

  If people mistakenly believe that they are already doing HPT and they are not, then they are suffering from overconfidence. They need to be shown that they would have to do this, this, and this to actually be HPT practitioners. They need to see that it is harder than they thought, or more involved than they thought, to do HPT, and they need to be told that they will need to invest more effort to actually develop an HPT solution to their business problem.

- *Oh, please! Not another "flavor of the month" process!* There have been so many proposals for improving performance in organizations—reengineering, management by objectives, total quality management, sociotechnical systems, organizational development, and so on—that some managers have become discouraged about even listening to information about one more system. If you mention "HPT," their first reaction is to bristle defensively and to turn off their receptiveness. They do not want to see another model or to hear more jargon. In short, they are not interested.

  To gain their interest, talk with them in plain English about what you are proposing to do. For example:

> You have been asked to provide conflict resolution training. You might say, "I'd like to look at this conflict situation in the department and see if there isn't something we can do to resolve it."

> When asked for teamwork training, you might suggest, "You know, training courses may not be the only way to increase a sense of teamwork. Let me talk with a few people who are on teams now and their managers to see if I can find out what

they don't know about functioning as teams and also whether there are other factors that may be discouraging the best teamwork practices."

When you are faced with a request for follow-up training on the XYZ process, you might say, "After talking with a sample of the people involved, I have discovered that they know how to follow the process. The reason they don't use it is because they are ridiculed by their peers if they do. Rather than providing more training in something that they already know, maybe we should look at how we might eliminate the ridicule and put some positive rewards in place."

You can practice HPT to your heart's content without telling anyone that the process you are using has a name. (Many people are not overly fond of either *performance* or *technology* as terms to describe this process. *Performance* makes them think of sports or race car engines, for example, and *technology* makes them think of computers or other sophisticated devices.) Save the technical terms for when you are talking with other performance technologists. If you suspect that your clients are jargon-shy, talk about "performance improvement efforts" or use some other phrase that doesn't require them to learn yet another new term.

Now we move on to barriers related to the environment.

• *We don't have permission to do HPT.* When the group's charter is to provide training programs and management does not express any interest in seeing HPT results, then there may not be any explicit permission to do anything differently. Management may not have heard of HPT and may therefore not be asking for it by name. You will need to use some of the strategies suggested elsewhere in the book to get management's permission to utilize HPT. Some of those strategies might include:

1. Do it anyway and don't tell anybody until you have some success stories. "Oh, by the way, we used HPT to complete that

project. See how it solved the real problem? And in this case it was faster and saved money, too."

2. Ask for permission one step at a time. "Would it be okay with you if I took a day or two to investigate the best way to solve this problem?" "We looked at this request for training and discovered that the issue can't be solved by training [or training alone]. It appears that this other solution would work better. Okay with you if we proceed?"

3. In a receptive environment, provide information about HPT and ask for permission to proceed. You can do it in tandem with your training efforts, if you have the resources for that approach. You can provide a plan to introduce HPT on a schedule that would work for your organization. Anticipate the change management issues and provide a plan to work with those from the start.

• *Although senior management supports the implementation of HPT, this is not widely known.* Even if your senior management has endorsed the use of HPT at your company, your internal customers may not know that this is so. Your potential internal customers may not have heard of HPT and therefore do not even know how or when to ask for it. You may need to work with your manager or the appropriate people in your company to encourage the publication of information about the support provided for HPT by senior management, what it is, and how and when to ask for it.

• *Our current processes would conflict with HPT processes.* If this objection comes up, you will certainly need to deal with it. This can be an issue of overlapping charters, different ways of proceeding, vocabulary differences, or perceived differences in processes.

For charter issues, work with the people who have overlapping charters to determine how to stay out of each other's way. For one thing, there are generally so many opportunities to improve performance that there is plenty of work to share. Seldom do people in any organization complain because they do not have enough to do.

However, it can be an issue to have HR, training, and organizational development professionals, for example, all tripping over each other while trying to solve the same problem. They may even begin to do redundant (wasteful) work.

When there are different ways of proceeding to solve business issues, your internal clients may become confused about who to turn to when they need assistance. They may find themselves in the situation of being courted by members of different organizations who are each touting their own processes and models as the best ones to solve performance improvement issues. If they all use different terms to describe similar processes, then their clients may want to give up in disgust.

So, try to work out who does what with other internal organizations. If possible, agree on one overarching model that provides guidance about which organization will tackle which kind of issue. Then call each other in to consult on issues where overlap is either desirable or unavoidable.

Often the biggest threat to HPT is political barriers. If you can map your HPT process onto a commonly used and central company process, then you may be able to talk about what you want to do in totally non-controversial terms. This process may be the new product (or service) development process, for example. This process probably has an investigation (analysis) phase, one or two phases for design and production (development), and a phase for product or service fulfillment (implementation). Map your ideal HPT process onto this central company process (after all, HPT and the company process just described involve four similar steps) and then talk about what you are doing in vocabulary that is common to business managers in your company. If they follow a systematic process for engineering or accounting or manufacturing, then they will respect you even more for having such a process for providing assistance with improving human performance.

• *We don't have positive consequences in place for solving problems using a systematic and systemic process.* If you can, put these positive consequences in place as soon as possible. Look for opportunities to reward people for following a systematic approach or for consider-ing the system within which their assigned problem resided. Make sure to let people know that you value such an approach and that it is worth rewarding. If your organization routinely rewards quick solutions, then look to see if people are less inclined to pursue a more thorough (and possibly more effective) approach. Try to elim-inate the mentality that rewards people who jump into the fray to solve emergencies that they created in the first place due to not thinking or planning ahead.

Make sure that you allow enough time to complete assignments in a systematic way rather than skimping on time, which encour-ages shortcuts that may result in a lot of activity but not much sub-stance. Even if an intervention results in a lot of noise or action (stirring the pot), it may or may not have provided the solution that was needed (cooking tasty soup). The best way to determine whether positive consequences are in order is to measure the busi-ness result of the intervention. Did it help the company to do some-thing better, faster, cheaper? Did it result in the company becoming a better place to work? If so, provide positive consequences. Do this even if the project was small and did not generate much fanfare. Do so in such a way that others will be encouraged to use HPT.

• *We have no feedback systems in place to let people know whether or not they are achieving the HPT results we are looking for.* If this proves to be a barrier, then you will need to let people know when they have contributed to the positive (or negative) results of a pro-ject. Your sponsors should find out what has changed for the better because they contracted with you to work on an issue. The people who provided input should find out that their input was helpful. Send them a thank-you and a statement about what they did that helped and how it helped, as applicable. People who worked on the project, whether from your department or another department, should be kept informed about what the results were and told what they did that was especially helpful to the project's success. Where there are issues about less-than-helpful efforts, these should be noted as well (probably privately with the individual or individuals involved) so that next time there will be improvement. Make sure, too, that your own management knows about the successes you've had, why they were successful, and who contributed to them.

• *We do not have a model or processes for doing HPT.* You will need to adopt, adapt, or create these processes for your department. You can use models and processes already created by others, change them to meet the needs of your environment and culture, or start over to create your own. It will be most helpful if you can agree on a model and processes to use throughout your organization. This will eliminate confusion and will enhance communication both within and outside of your department. For help with determining what your model or processes should be, see Chapter Two.

• *We have no tools for doing HPT.* If HPT is new to your organization, you will probably not have any tools in place to help practitioners move through the process. "Tools" in this case might be job aids, including decision aids and checklists; sample questions to modify for different situations; talking points for different stages of the process for describing HPT to potential clients; copies of the model; and so on. If you introduce HPT in gradual stages, you can assign tool making to the pioneer performance consultants in your department. Whenever they work on a project, they should look for ideas for tools that will help them and others to make the work go smoother, easier, quicker, or more consistently. Assign them the task of making one or more tools that others might use as they complete each of their initial projects. As you bring new performance consultants on board, determine what tools they need and help them to find or create them. Eventually you will develop a complete set of tools for your team of performance consultants to use.

Implementing Solutions to Your HPT Barriers

When you discover barriers to implementing HPT in your company, as we have just illustrated, make a list of those barriers and organize them by these three categories: knowledge and skills, motivation, and environment. Then make a list of the solutions you believe will eliminate those barriers. Note interdependencies between your barriers and solutions. For example, do you need some examples of success stories before you develop your pitch for the executive team? Can you work out charter issues with other groups at the same time that you are providing training in HPT for multiple audiences? If you fix one thing without fixing something else, will there be negative consequences?

Once you have your list of solutions, you will need to arrange for their design, development, and implementation. For each solution related to a barrier that exists today, determine who you will need to help implement the solution, what budget will be required, and what the time line should be for putting it in place (See Figure 7.4).

Some of the barriers you identified may be potential rather than existing barriers: they may or may not appear until partway through the implementation process. Determine how you will monitor for those potential barriers. What clues will you look for that will indicate that you should do something to validate and then eliminate those barriers? Should you assign someone on your staff to assist with monitoring for these clues? If you have an idea about solutions to these potential barriers already, be sure to note what you think the solutions will be and how you think they should be put in place.

Figure 7.4. Implementing Your Solutions.

Each of your solutions may represent a small project in itself. If one or more of the solutions are new to you—for example, designing a motivation or feedback system—then you may need to obtain help from someone who knows how to create that particular type of solution.

Solution Implementation			
Select solution set	Design interventions	Develop interventions	Implement solutions

Summary

In this chapter we have focused on applying the process of HPT to your company to enhance its readiness and ability to implement HPT. Using the human performance system as an organizing principle, we have systematically looked at some sample positive and negative forces for HPT, derived some possible barriers, and suggested some ways to validate apparent barriers. Categorizing existing barriers into those related to a lack of knowledge and skill, to motivation problems, or to environmental problems can suggest the types of solutions that will eliminate those barriers.

Here are some main points from this chapter:

- You can use the HPT process to help guide your implementation of HPT at your company.

- Define your goals for implementing HPT at your company and decide how you will know that you have achieved them.

- Use the human performance system to identify current and potential barriers to implementing HPT.

- Validate your suspected barriers to make sure that your assumptions are correct.

- Make a list of your proposed solutions and determine what resources you will need for putting them in place.

- Orchestrate the timing of your solutions to maximize their effectiveness.

Now that we've looked at the bigger picture of implementing HPT in a company, we go into more detail about how to implement it with the group of people who will be the HPT practitioners in your organization. We look at issues that may occur within your organization and at ways to solve those issues.

8

Making the Transition to HPT Within Your Department

In this chapter we will help you to take a close look at your department to determine the best way to enable HPT practices there. "The best way" will depend, of course, on many things. The goals, climate, and overall system of the larger organization will be important factors, as discussed in Chapter Seven. But your department will have a number of factors closer to you that you will also want to address. These factors will vary depending on your current position and the goals and structure of your department.

Your Current Position

Are you making the change to HPT by yourself? Do you run a department? To whom do you report? The answers to these questions can be critical in determining the extent of your ability to make the transition to HPT. Let's assume, for the sake of argument, that there are three levels of authority held by training professionals who might want to switch to HPT: individual contributor, first-level manager (someone who manages individual contributors), and second-level manager or director (someone who manages first-level managers). Within each of these authority levels there will be considerable variance in how much control you have over your own work or that of your subordinates, if you have them. A typical hierarchy is shown in Figure 8.1.

Figure 8.1. Typical Hierarchical Organization Structure for Training Organizations.

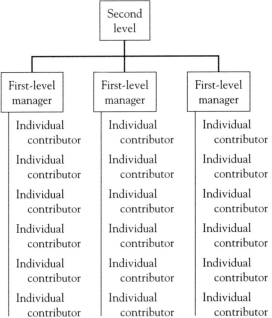

In addition to differences in levels of authority, there will be some variance in where the idea to move to HPT originates. For example, you could be the only person in your organization who has heard about HPT, and you might have made your own decision about wanting to become a performance consultant. Or someone from the executive team might have mandated that all performance improvement professionals and all managers should acquire at least the rudiments of HPT.

Depending on your position and your motivation for moving to HPT, you might find it helpful to map out the scope of the change you wish to undertake. If you are a lone individual contributor who has no training colleagues but who reports to a line manager or a human resource manager, consider whether you want to be making the switch all by yourself. It may be helpful and supportive to have other people making the transition with you. Who else might you influence? Who else might want to learn and make changes alongside you? You could enlist others who might be willing to make the transition with you, for example, your manager, other people who report to your manager, the quality folks in the next department, or other training professionals in another department.

If you are an individual contributor in a department of training professionals, then your colleagues and your manager may be interested in making the transition. They may want to go slowly, one project or analysis effort at a time, but they may join you nonetheless.

Training managers may wish to incubate HPT quietly in their own organization before taking it to their managers for review. They may wish to work closely with their staffs to teach them aspects of HPT for each new project that offers a promising HPT opportunity. Or if they have a staff member experienced in conducting HPT projects, they might assign that person to work with others to help them learn how to apply HPT. Managing up and sideways will be important. Make sure to keep your manager and your peers informed about the successes you experience with HPT, and also let them know why doing things differently provided an advantage over some of the standard operating procedures of the past.

How Big a Chunk Do You Want?

Before setting more detailed goals for implementing HPT, you should map out the territory where you wish to engage. How much of the process do you want to own or conduct? The world of HPT spans a wide range of roles, including those of sponsor, project or change manager, analyst, and solution developer. If you are an individual contributor, one of the simplest approaches to HPT is to approach each training request with an HPT mind-set. When issues that cannot be solved by training arise, you would notify your client that you have discovered some environmental or motivational barriers to performance that may prevent their goals from being reached. You would gracefully decline requests for training when training would not solve the problem. A more comprehensive approach would be to become a performance consultant, conducting a performance analysis in response to most requests, verifying root causes of business problems, managing the entire process of implementing both training and nontraining solutions, and then measuring results.

As a training manager you also have choices about how much you want your department to be engaged with HPT. At a simple level, you (or designated staff members) might screen all requests for training, identify the business issues, and make a quick assessment about whether training (or training alone) is likely to provide the intended result. You could accept responsibility for providing training and refer your client to other performance improvement specialists for additional solutions. A more complex change would be to become an HPT department, taking responsibility for solving a wide range of business problems, staffing your department with performance consultants and solution developers, and managing requests for assistance with human performance issues from analysis to evaluation.

If you are a second-level manager, overseeing a number of training departments or several departments offering different types of performance improvement solutions, then you can choose a similar range of involvement with HPT. On the one hand, you can encourage a systems approach to requests for service coupled with advice to the client about a potential range of necessary solutions. On the other hand, you can reorganize your entire organization to provide a proactive approach to business issues and to systematically handle all requests for service with HPT, as required.

In addition, you may wish to consider whether there is a likelihood that other performance improvement professionals (for example, in human resources or quality) and/or the managers at your company should or would want to learn how to look at things with an HPT mind-set. This would entail applying a systems view and using a systematic, data-driven approach to solving problems.

Whatever your level of authority, you will need to examine the resources available to help you. What role should you play? What roles should others in your department play? Are there people in other departments who should play a part in some or all of the HPT projects you engage in? If Mr. Client from Department X wants help with a problem, should you contact the local human resource representative and bring her into the analysis? When you think the best solution will result in a change of organizational structure, should you call in an organizational development specialist for a consultation? When you need an ergonomic solution and the one ergonomic specialist in your company is too swamped with other work to provide it, what should you do? Should you hire an external ergonomic specialist but ask the internal specialist to be on the review team for the design, development, and evaluation of that solution?

In the early stages of an HPT project, ask yourself questions such as the following:

1. Who is available to work on HPT projects whom I can persuade or assign to work on projects?
2. What expertise is needed and where is it to be found?
3. Who has the goals, latitude, or permission to work on these projects?
4. What funding issues need to be considered?
5. Who has the charter to solve the presenting issue?

For more about the skills required to conduct HPT projects, see Chapter Nine.

Setting Goals for Implementing HPT

What, specifically, do you want to do with HPT in your position or with your department? Goals will vary considerably for different people, in different positions in the organizational hierarchy, and in different departments. You may want to brainstorm a list of goals. Here are some ideas to get you started:

Individual Goals

Obtain permission to do performance consulting.

Change my focus to obtaining business results.

Conduct performance analyses.

Make data-driven decisions.

Make recommendations to create solutions other than training.

Manage the development and implementation of solution sets.

Partner with other performance improvement professionals to create solutions.

Department Goals

Receive requests for systemic solutions.

Offer a broader range of analysis and solutions.

Change our performance metrics to include business results.

Approach all presenting problems with an HPT mind-set.

Develop a proactive stance toward solving business problems and opportunities.

Create models, processes, and tools for engaging in performance consulting.

Obtain the funding and staff to enable the practice of HPT.

After you have brainstormed your initial list, you can check it against the criteria we have talked about already: your role, authority, initiation, and resources. Your first pass at the items on your list can be made by looking at the following questions:

1. Is this the kind of goal that I can influence or carry out in my current role as an individual contributor, manager, or director?

2. What kind of authority or influence do I have to make changes in my current performance goals or in the charter of my department? Is it reasonable to think that I have or can obtain permission to tackle this goal?

3. Does the initiation for this goal come only from me, from my management, or from some other source? Will I need to persuade influential people that this goal is worth pursuing?

4. Can I achieve this goal alone, or will I be working with a team, my staff, my management, or the members of other organizations?

Based on your answers to these questions, you may wish to add, delete, or modify some of the goals on your list to make them more achievable. In addition, you may want to refine them to make them more clear and to reduce ambiguity about what you want to achieve. To help do this, you can conduct a *goal analysis* for each goal that is still on your list. Mager (1997) suggests a five-step process for refining goals:

1. Write down an approximation of your goal (it can be quite fuzzy at this point). You may have done this already.

2. Describe the performance you would need to see to believe that the goal has been achieved. Brainstorming is desirable at this step; you'll edit your list in Step 3.

3. Refine your list. Eliminate redundancies and unimportant items. If some of your performance statements are not clear, then repeat Steps 1 and 2 for those items.

4. Write each performance statement as a complete sentence. Include a standard (for example, quality, quantity, cost, time) to indicate how you'll know that the performance is satisfactory.

5. Review your list of performance statements to determine if they are both necessary and sufficient to describe the achievement of your goal.

Actually writing out your goals using this process can be especially helpful. See Exhibit 8.1 for a sample end result of a goal to conduct performance analyses. For more details and examples about how to follow this process, see *Goal Analysis*, by Robert Mager (1997).

Taking Stock

Once you have identified the specific goals you want to tackle with HPT, then you should take stock of your ability to achieve them. Which of the goals are already being achieved? Which ones are achievable simply by deciding to do them? For which goals will you or others need additional knowledge, skills, tools, money, time, people, partnerships, or permission to attempt?

Conduct a tools checkup. What do you have that will help you? Do you already have models, templates, job aids, and references? For some goals, you may need to assemble, modify, or create tools for your own or others' use. Make a list of the things you will need. If you need help, turn to an expert to make the list and to acquire HPT tools.

Look at your goals and give some thought to how you expect things to go for you, your team, your manager, your manager's manager, and others. Do you think these goals will be easy to achieve? Will some of them prove difficult? Make some notes about your thoughts. As appropriate, compare your thinking with that of others, for example, colleagues, staff members, or your manager. Make note of the goals that seem to provide the biggest challenges, then be sure to give them special attention.

Also, remember that the goals you have adopted may be too comprehensive to achieve overnight. Which parts of the goals can you tackle now? Can you implement them in a phased approach? If you divide the goals into achievable chunks, then you may be able to adopt one project at a time or one section of the goals at a time. If you try to implement everything at once, your efforts may not provide positive results.

Exhibit 8.1. Sample Results of a Goal Analysis.

Conduct Performance Analyses

Performance consultants will conduct performance analyses as defined by the following performance statements:

1. State the business issue in terms of a problem that needs to be solved or an opportunity that can be realized.
2. Describe the intended results in terms of performance metrics that would indicate that the issue has been solved.
3. Describe the current performance related to the business issue in terms of measurable results.
4. Describe the performance that would be necessary to meet the business goal in terms of desired results.
5. List any gaps between current performance and necessary performance, including statements of quality, quantity, time, and money, as appropriate.
6. Describe the root causes of the gaps in terms of knowledge and skills, motivation, and environmental issues.
7. Recommend solutions that will eliminate the identified barriers to performance.

One-Page Briefs

If you want to take a closer look at specific areas that may or may not need to be changed before HPT can be implemented in your department, creating one-page briefs can be most helpful. Briefs will help you to get yourself organized and to check for alignment of inputs, processes, and outputs. Briefs are organized around the human performance system shown in Figure 2.1. You can fill them out for a given job, task, process, or goal. They can help you to see where there are areas that need improvement. You may wish to include the following headings from the human performance system in your briefs:

- *Performance.* What do you want the end result to be? How will you measure it (for example, in terms of cost, quality, or quantity)?

Describe how you will recognize that the results you were looking for have been achieved. (You can use input from your goal analysis to describe performance.)

- *Input.* What expectations, people, knowledge, skills, attitudes, and so on will be required to achieve the desired performance? Note what will trigger starting the actions necessary to achieve the desired performance.

- *Environment.* What information, tools, equipment, processes, and conditions must be in place to support the desired performance?

- *Consequences.* What rewards, incentives, recognition, perceptions about status, and increased or decreased responsibility are in place or should be in place to support the achievement of the desired performance?

- *Process.* Describe what will need to be done to achieve the desired performance. This may include the procedures required for completing a number of tasks.

- *Feedback.* Describe what indicators you expect to see for success or for areas where improvement is needed. Feedback should be delivered to performers, as appropriate, as they complete their work and again once their work is done and the results of their efforts are known.

We provide two examples of one-page briefs. They amplify the goal analyzed earlier: to conduct performance analyses. The first version is presented in Exhibit 8.2 and follows a linear format with each of the organizing principles from the human performance system as headings.

The second version, this one in a nonlinear format, is presented in Figure 8.2. The fastest and probably the best way to draw these "clustered" briefs is by hand. If you want to create a more formal brief, for example, to share with management, you can use a software program to draw more uniform circles and to type the words. It is much quicker, however, to draw these nonlinear briefs without a computer, so it may be more beneficial to start off using a pen or pencil and paper. One benefit of using the nonlinear format is that you can create briefs on your own, or you can use huge pieces of paper and draw your briefs

Exhibit 8.2. A One-Page Brief on Conducting Performance Analyses.

Conducting Performance Analyses

Performance. At the end of this process, we will have a list of solutions that will address the verified barriers to achieving business results.

Input. We will need to know precisely what business issues have triggered the request for the analysis and what our client will accept as evidence that the issues have been resolved. We will need access to our client and to a cross-section of people who have an impact on or who are affected by the business issue. We will also need expertise in the conduct of performance analyses and expertise about the expected results of a variety of possible solutions to the business issue.

Environment. We need information about people, processes, and organization surrounding and involved with the business issue. Also important are performance consulting tools, models, and processes, as well as general office equipment and supplies, meeting rooms, and a budget for necessary travel, telephone charges, copy charges, and delivery services.

Process. A flexible, documented, and step-by-step performance analysis process that follows a well-accepted HPT model should be used in conjunction with a project management process to assist with finishing the analysis to specifications, on time, and within budget.

Consequences. Performance consulting represents an increase in responsibility, visibility, and impact as compared with training positions. The completion of a performance analysis that meets our specifications should be celebrated as a major milestone achievement.

Feedback. The manager of a performance consultant should review the process and results of a performance analysis and be sure to communicate with the consultant about what went well and what can be improved. If process or other improvements are discovered, these should be communicated to other consultants and documented for future use.

Figure 8.2. The Start of a Nonlinear Brief.

together with others on your team. To create this kind of brief, write a few words describing the task, process, or goal in the middle of a horizontal piece of paper and put a circle around it (see Figure 8.2).

Once you have put your main thought in the middle of the paper, write "performance" a little bit above the first circle, draw a circle around that word, and connect the two circles with a line. Write words or short phrases that describe the performance you are looking for. Draw circles around each of these words or phrases and draw lines connecting those circles to "performance." For an example of this stage of the brief, see Figure 8.3. You can elaborate on any of the descriptors of "performance" by adding more words or phrases. Link them as you wish.

Add the additional main elements of the human performance system: input, environment, consequences, process, feedback. Add words or phrases to describe the conditions of each element. For an example of this stage of the brief, see Figure 8.4.

Figure 8.3. Filling in a Nonlinear Brief.

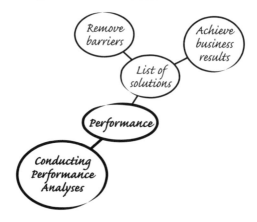

Figure 8.4. A Completed Nonlinear Brief.

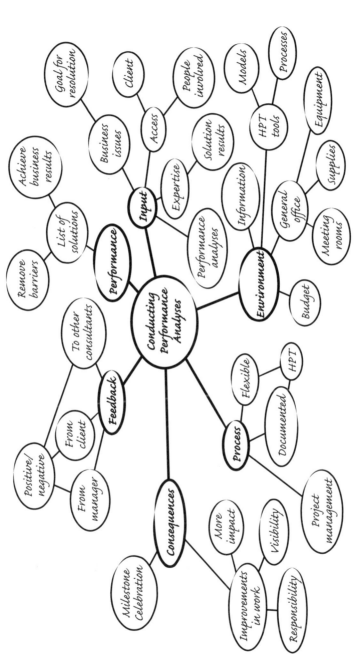

When you have finished thinking of ideas related to the human performance system, you can stop. More likely, you will run out of room before you run out of ideas. You can continue on another page by choosing a particularly rich idea from the first page and making it the main topic of the next page. Use this process to determine what you already know about the issue you have chosen to write into a brief. By now it should be fairly clear to you which areas call for more information and which areas need to be improved.

Once you are finished with your handwritten cluster brief, you can make it more formal by transforming it into the linear format already suggested. But if the brief is just for your own use or for the use of the team that created it, you can leave it in its handwritten form.

Creating New Roles

Now that you have created the specific goals you have for adding HPT to your job or department, you will need to look at the roles that will be required for meeting those goals. One person can fulfill more than one role. Here are some roles to consider:

• *HPT sponsor.* Your sponsor may change from project to project. As we mentioned previously, every time you embark on an HPT project you will need someone to sponsor it. Often this someone will be your internal client or your manager. Your clients do not need to be able to describe or understand HPT; they only need to allow you to investigate a business problem and to recommend or provide solutions for solving it.

• *HPT champion.* Your champion will be primarily responsible for spreading the word about the benefits of HPT. This person (there may be more than one) will most likely be in your department. He or she will be giving presentations about the benefits of HPT once you have some success stories to share.

• *Performance consultant.* This is a person who practices performance technology. It will not be necessary for everyone in your department to be a performance consultant. The person in this role makes an agreement with the client to provide services, determines what must be accomplished, and ensures that the business issue is resolved to the client's satisfaction. For more complicated projects, ones in which multiple HPT resources are assigned, it is a good idea to have a lead performance consultant on every project. This lead consultant sets direction with the client and takes responsibility for the overall results of the project.

• *Performance analyst.* A performance analyst for a project will be in charge of defining the problem or issues that need to be addressed, determining the gaps in performance, making sure the root cause analysis is conducted, and recommending solutions for eliminating barriers to performance.

• *Root cause analyst.* Determining root causes may provide a special challenge in some projects. The lead consultant or performance analyst may wish to call in an expert to determine the root causes of the identified gaps in performance. Someone from quality may be able to help with this part of the process.

• *Solution developer.* Once the necessary solutions to the performance problem have been identified, someone needs to develop them. You may need an instructional designer to develop training or job aids, a compensation analyst to change a wage structure, an organizational development specialist to help restructure the organization, or an ergonomics professional to design solutions to computer or desk configuration problems.

• *Solution implementers.* Many solutions, once developed, require one or more people to carry them out or to put them in motion. These people may be trainers to deliver training, ergonomics field workers to provide assessments, or managers to participate in making changes in their organizations' structures or to follow through with wage adjustments from a new compensation plan.

• *Partners.* You may not have enough people (or people with the right skills) available in your department to take on all the roles a given project will require. Thus you may need to call on people from other organizations, either inside or outside your company, to

act as partners to the members of your department in implementing a specific HPT project. This may necessitate developing some
new ways of goal setting, consequence management, and feedback
delivery for people both inside and outside your department.

• *HPT consultant or mentor.* One or more people inside or outside your department may be needed to answer questions, provide
guidance, or assist in solving problems that arise during the course of
a HPT project.

• *Project manager.* HPT projects can become complex. One person will need to ensure that time lines are met, that the scope of
the project is well defined, that the goals of the project are met, that
the budget is not exceeded, and that the people playing various roles
and working together will have such a positive experience that they
would be willing to work together again.

• *Facilitator.* When focus groups are required as part of the
analysis process, someone will need to facilitate gathering information from the participants. The facilitator's role includes managing
difficult participants, drawing out ideas from reticent participants,
and generally ensuring that the best information is captured from
the group.

• *Change adviser.* HPT interventions can change how, why,
when, where, or with whom work is done. Whenever change is
involved, people may have negative reactions to the change. Even
if the change is widely perceived as positive, difficulties in making
the change can occur. Someone should be managing the change
process to ensure that the change as proposed will have the desired
result and will transfer to common practice in the workplace.

For every project you may wish to look at this list of roles (and
perhaps other roles as well) and determine which ones are necessary to complete the project successfully. (See Exhibit 8.3 for a summary.) You will need to determine who can play the necessary roles.
For many projects, one person will play the majority of these roles.
Where that person will often need help is with the development
and implementation of a variety of solutions. Few people have

expertise in designing or implementing more than a few kinds of interventions. In addition, where there are large-scale implementation efforts, more than one person may be required to meet the implementation plans.

Responding to Requests

As part of a training organization, you may have considerable experience responding to requests for training. Your organization probably already has a process for handling such requests, which may include assigning someone to collect information about the problem to be solved, analyzing gaps to determine what training (if any) is needed to solve the problem, and asking a training specialist to find an existing training program or to create a new one. In responding to requests for training, the focus is on determining how (and whether) training can solve a particular business problem.

Now that you are moving to HPT, you will need to create a new process to respond to requests. This new process should include listening carefully to the request, finding out what solution (if any) the client has in mind, gathering some information about the business issues to be solved, and then contracting with the client to investigate further. The investigation (performance analysis) should be assigned to someone who can move through the process to determine what is getting in the way of the performance required to meet the client's business needs. When responding to requests from an HPT point of view, the focus should be on determining how to eliminate barriers to performance. No definite plans, whether for creating training programs or other particular kinds of solutions, should be put in place before the root causes are validated.

In the absence of a defined problem but in response to a desire to improve performance in a specific area, you may find that you are engaging in a *proactive* HPT project. For example, your company may have high customer satisfaction ratings but management may still want to increase customer satisfaction, as measured by Survey

Exhibit 8.3. Summary of HPT Roles.

Role	Responsibility
HPT sponsor	Paves the way for the project. Usually involves permission, access to resources, and budget.
HPT champion	Spreads the word about the benefits of HPT.
Performance consultant	Practices HPT in general.
Performance analyst	Practices HPT, specifically those parts of the HPT process from defining a problem through recommending a solution set.
Root-Cause analyst	Identifies and validates the root causes to specified performance problems.
Solution developer	Creates one or more interventions identified in the solution set.
Solution implementer	Organizes or delivers the interventions once they have been developed.
Partners	People from outside your organization who add specific capabilities to the project.
HPT consultant or mentor	Provides HPT guidance to individuals, departments, or projects.
Project manager	Ensures that timelines, scope, budget, and relationships are managed.
Facilitator	Runs focus groups, as needed.
Change adviser	Assists with managing the change process.

X, by 20 percent. Or a particular department may wish to have a performance analysis done to determine how it can best be prepared for expected market conditions three years from now. In either case, the response will be the same: carefully define the business issue (in this case in positive terms), work with your client to determine the scope (boundaries) of the request, and then assign someone to implement the HPT methodology described in this chapter.

Two issues that may plague you during your first HPT projects might be (1) getting permission to engage in HPT practices and (2) a tradition of being in a responding role. Support for getting permission to do HPT is provided at some length in Chapter Five. Assuming more of a leadership role will require confidence and practice. One way to build confidence is to include your client in the discovery of a new way of proceeding. Another is to bring in someone to help you with setting direction with the client. This person can provide a model, some coaching, and support as you observe, practice, and then engage on your own.

A last issue that may come into play when you receive a request for service is your own uncertainty about when to use HPT. It's easy to address this issue. When should you use HPT? Always. Once you are accustomed to looking at things from a systems point of view, you will always do some form of performance consulting whenever you are working on a performance improvement project. Even if you are doing a training analysis, you will zero in on the business problem. Your gap analyses will go beyond what is needed for inclusion in a training solution. Thus your recommendations about solutions will be more robust and more systemic.

Creating New Success Criteria

If your training department is like most others, the success criteria currently in place do not support HPT. Usually the goals in place encourage you to persuade large numbers of employees to attend training classes.

So in addition to learning how to do HPT, individual contributors and managers in the training function will need to set new goals and develop rewards that match their new goals. Once you have some small successes, you will need to talk with your manager about the value HPT can bring to the department and the company. And you will need to enlist help from that person to change some of your goals and any commensurate rewards to line up with the benefits good performance in HPT will bring the organization. This may involve looking at numbers of students and numbers of training courses differently and arranging different metrics for training services. It may include goals related to solving the business issues clients bring to you, whether they originate as training requests or not.

Developing Allies

To implement HPT you will be using a new form of analysis, one that looks at the entire system. You'll be including a root cause analysis process in your investigations. You may be recommending some noninstructional solutions that are unfamiliar. All of this may cause some discomfort because it is new.

Developing relationships with others, that is, finding allies, may make everything go a lot smoother. Just having someone to talk with about the new process or the next step in an HPT project can provide a much-needed sounding board. Often when explaining something out loud to a sympathetic ally you may suddenly have a better idea or realize a flaw in your original thinking. It is much better to have this happen in an informal setting with a colleague than in your client's high-powered staff meeting where you've been invited to explain your next steps.

In addition to making sure that you have an ally to listen to your thinking, you will need to make other allies in your organization. Make a list of people to engage in meetings or other forms of communication about HPT. For example, you will want to hold one-on-one meetings with your manager, your peers, and your employees (if you have them). These meetings should include informational or coaching sessions, development discussions, and goal setting. On a larger scale, you may wish to participate in or hold staff meetings and larger department meetings, if applicable, to nail down your model, tools, philosophy, goals, and vision.

Outside your organization, you may find it helpful to develop allies who are performance consultants in other companies or who are professors who concentrate on HPT. As long as you keep any confidentiality issues in careful check, these external colleagues can serve as helpful allies by listening to your problems, venturing helpful thoughts, and coaching you toward greater success.

Some of your most valuable allies may be your past clients. They can provide referrals, advice, and sponsorship for future projects and developments in your HPT practice.

Summary

In this chapter, we have looked at what you need to focus on to get yourself and your department ready to implement HPT. You will need to do a fair amount of investigation and planning to determine exactly how you want to implement HPT in your current situation. There are a variety of angles to consider, including your position, the level of authority from which the request comes for the change to HPT, whether there is an internal community that can develop together in the practice of HPT, where to get help for any parts of the process that your department is not yet ready to tackle, how much of the process to embrace, and how pervasive the practice should be.

Here are some main points from this chapter:

- You need to plan for the timing, practice, and staffing of your HPT effort.

- Creating goals for yourself and your department can be attended to in a systematic way that will provide clarity

about what you want to do and hints about what will
need to be improved before HPT can be successfully
implemented.

- One-page briefs can help you to examine your goals
from the various aspects of the human performance
system to give you a quick look at your strengths
and weaknesses.

- The way you and your department respond to requests
for training or other services will change focus, moving
from how to provide the requested training to how to
solve the business issue.

- The number and complexity of roles people play in
fulfilling customer requests will expand.

- Once you have established HPT as a way to improve
the effectiveness and efficiency of your company's business, you will need to negotiate a change in goals and
rewards for yourself and/or your department.

- Internal and external allies can provide invaluable
services by acting as advocates for HPT, sounding
boards for your thoughts, mentors, and more.

The next chapter contains information on how individuals can
acquire the knowledge and skills necessary to practice HPT.
Although there is a natural progression from instructional designer
to performance consultant, the transition can't be made simply by
reading one book or attending one workshop. Acquiring knowledge
and skills over time, deliberate practice, and adequate feedback are
the three minimal requirements for developing into a performance
consultant. With a reasonable amount of effort, a good development
plan, and adequate experience, most training professionals should
be able to make the transition.

9

How to Develop HPT Professionals Within Your Organization

No matter how much strategic thinking you've done or which organizational or motivational barriers to implementing HPT you've uncovered and figured out how to solve, at the end of the day you will need to have qualified HPT practitioners: performance consultants who can deliver on the promise and practice of HPT. In this chapter, we look at the general and specific capabilities that performance consultants must have. We also look at creating short-term and long-term plans for their development.

To help your performance consultants to develop HPT knowledge and skills, do the following:

• Determine which roles should be played by which individuals. (See Chapter Eight.)
• Decide which knowledge and skills are required for each role.
• Assess the knowledge and skills match between individuals and roles.
• Complete development plans for yourself and for each person in your department, as appropriate.

The first step in completing your plan should be to determine which part or parts of the performance consulting role each person will play. As we noted in Chapter Eight, one person may engage in one or more parts of an HPT project. For example, she could manage the entire project, conduct the performance analysis, and develop one or more types of solutions. If you create performance goals or a job description that describes the results you are looking for from each person, then it will be easier for you to determine what knowledge and skills each individual will need.

Determine what knowledge and which skills the future performance consultant already possesses. Then determine what role or roles that consultant is likely to play during the next twelve months. Which skills will be essential for this person to acquire? Which skills can be augmented by other people, either internal to your team or brought in from the outside? Make plans to leverage those situations in which a new performance consultant is being assisted by someone whose HPT skills are well developed. Be sure to create many opportunities for demonstrations, modeling, and coaching so that the new performance consultant can acquire more knowledge and skills by shadowing and learning from more experienced colleagues.

In the next section we describe an array of skills essential to the tasks associated with performance consulting. No one person can be a master of all these skills, but each performance consultant should strive to master one or more of them. You may want to encourage different people in your department to focus on acquiring and/or developing different skills, as appropriate, so that they can work together as a team to tackle performance consulting problems that call for all the necessary skills.

General HPT Knowledge and Skills

We describe the following eight general areas of capabilities that are essential for a performance consultant:

1. Business focus
2. A systemic, systematic approach
3. Strong interpersonal skills
4. Consulting skills

5. Project management skills

6. Change management skills

7. Teamwork

8. Working with experts

Business Focus

With performance consulting, the focus often shifts from fulfilling a training request or adding additional courses to solving business issues. Generally the solution of a business problem involves an improvement in cost, quality, quantity, or timeliness.

Along with having a business rationale before recommending a new intervention, performance consultants should be able to speak intelligently about their company's business. With an external focus, performance consultants should be able to speak fluently about their company's products and/or services, markets, and major customers. With an internal focus, they should be able to describe the major organizations within the company and the major processes used to create products and services to meet customers' needs. Having little or no knowledge of the business your company is in, the products and services you provide to your marketplace, or the organization and processes used to meet customer needs will be a surefire way to destroy your credibility from the start.

Using instructional design or HPT jargon rather than plain language to describe your processes to your customer might well indicate to him that you do not understand his business. After listening to the "pitches" of a number of performance improvement professionals from different disciplines as they describe their models and use their specific language, senior managers sometimes lose patience. Describing your process and their situation in business terms rather than in technical HPT terms may go a long way toward establishing clear communications and obtaining the client's permission to proceed. It will also assist you at each stage of the process as you describe your findings, make recommendations for solutions, and report the results of your project. See Chapter Two for more about using plain language with your clients.

A Systemic, Systematic Approach

Looking at the system within which a business issue arises is an essential part of performance consulting. As we have noted throughout this book, *systems thinking* means taking an ecological approach to problems. The skills involved here include the following:

- Checking to see which elements of a system are related to each other.

- Determining which inputs, processes, and outputs from one element of a system interact with other elements of that system.

- Predicting which parts of a system are likely to change when another part of the system is changed.

- Using the human performance system as a helpful framework for determining where making one change may affect other elements of a system. Sometimes these interrelationships will not seem obvious or necessary at first glance (or without systems thinking).

Systems thinking often results in developing a set of solutions to a problem instead of just one solution. Of course, sometimes a single intervention will solve a problem. For example, improving the feedback provided to a particular group of employees could be all that is needed. However, in many other instances multiple interventions will be required to obtain sustainable performance that will meet business needs. For example, if the people in a particular department do not know how to do something, training may be required. Then, if they don't know what they are expected to do with what they learned in training, their goals may need to be changed. Finally, if they are not being suitably rewarded for doing something new that they learned in training, then their performance rewards may need to be realigned.

Doing things systematically means following a number of essential steps. In the case of HPT, your performance consultants will need to become fluent with the human performance system and the HPT model. At a minimum, they will need to identify the business issue, determine what success will look like, figure out what is causing the gaps in current performance, recommend solutions, see that they are implemented, and verify that the business issue has been solved. At first your performance consultants will most likely follow these steps in a linear fashion. As they become more fluent with the process, they will often perform some of these steps in a more iterative way. With practice, some aspects of certain problems will cue automatic expertise that will quickly sift through the human performance system and the HPT model to pinpoint the likely root causes of an issue. Verifying those root causes will still be an important step, but even this step will become easier with experience. Although there is no substitute for including the essential elements of performance consulting, over time an experienced performance consultant will be able to follow the process much more quickly than will a novice.

Strong Interpersonal Skills

Conducting an HPT project requires a number of interactions with a variety of people at different levels in an organization. In one workshop we conducted, a student proclaimed, when hearing about the process involved in conducting a performance analysis, "Oh, no, this means I'll have to sit down and talk with my manager's manager." She was intimidated by this possibility because she was unsure of her capacity to meet one-on-one with a senior manager. Performance consultants need to develop the ability to interact with people who may be several levels above them on the organization chart. In truth, directors, general managers, and vice presidents are often the clients or sponsors of HPT projects. In addition to inter-acting with people higher (or lower) in the hierarchy, performance consultants will interact with people from diverse functional back-grounds, for example, people from finance, engineering, marketing, sales, manufacturing, facilities, and information resources. Just about anyone in the company may cross paths with the performance con-sultant as part of a performance consulting project.

Moreover, not only will the performance consultant gather and share information with a wide variety of people at different levels from different departments, but he or she will also be involved in various types of interactions, including the following:

- Communicating the status of a project

- Staying on track

- Presenting ideas persuasively

- Selling a concept or approach

- Holding an exploratory discussion to search for infor-mation one-on-one or in groups

- Managing focus groups

- Using appropriate and nonbiasing questioning tech-niques (for example, asking open-ended and closed questions effectively, asking non-leading questions, and so on)

- Fostering inquiry and advocacy as appropriate to fur-ther the goals of an interaction

- Focusing a conversation to gather information effi-ciently while making sure that participants neither go off on tangents nor neglect to share information criti-cal to the project's success

- Defusing potential emotional reactions to problems while gathering needed information

- Dealing constructively with contention

If your potential performance consultants tend to arouse emotional reactions in their coworkers, dwell on the negative aspects of a situation, have little political savvy, or drift into conversational irrelevancies, then they need some serious coaching or other interventions to tune up their interpersonal skills.

Consulting Skills

Performance consultants must develop consulting skills if they do not already have them. They must be able to enter into a discussion with a potential client, determine what services and results the client requires, and formulate a contract with that client. The performance consultant will then use the HPT process to conduct the work of the HPT engagement.

As performance consultants work through the steps of the HPT model, they will also use consulting skills to maintain contact with the client, communicate the status of the project as appropriate, and negotiate any changes in the contract, such as changes to the time line or scope of the project. When the project is wrapping up, the performance consultant will need to complete the contract with the client, provide support and maintenance as required, and terminate the engagement. There are several excellent books on consulting skills, including Peter Block's *Flawless Consulting* (1981) and Geoffrey Bellman's *The Consultant's Calling* (1992).

Project Management

The performance consultant will need project management skills to see each project through from beginning to end. Project management skills overlap with the skills required for consulting and change management. As a project begins, the performance consultant will need to define the relationship with the project sponsor (and make sure there is one). The performance consultant will need to define the HPT project, including how to make trade-offs between time lines, cost, and project specifications. Planning a project is a complex skill that should not be underestimated; its many facets include creating a work breakdown structure and a schedule estimation, determining the interdependencies in the schedule, optimizing the schedule, and resourcing the project (Fuller, 1997). The performance consultant will need to analyze risks to project completion and engage in contingency planning to help minimize those risks. Vendor management may be required with some projects. The performance consultant may be called on to write requests for proposals and to select and manage vendors. Overall, the performance consultant will need to manage the entire project, making sure that its requirements are being fulfilled, that the people working on the project are aware of their roles and responsibilities, that the timing and scheduling of the project is going according to plan, that the budget is within limits, and that all necessary communications to make things run smoothly are conducted.

Change Management

In every HPT project where interventions are specified and implemented, a change will occur that represents a new way of working (Dormant, 1992). To those involved, the change may appear to be insignificant, or it may seem quite drastic. Resistance to change may prevent the targeted business issue from being resolved in what would otherwise be a successful HPT project. To foster an environment that is conducive to change and to shepherd a given intervention or strategy through the change process includes at a minimum the following necessary skills and actions:

- Enlisting the support and cooperation of sponsors, advocates, early adopters, team members, and others involved with the change.

- Recognizing and minimizing weaknesses in an intervention (alas, none of them are perfect).

- Recognizing the stages of change and employing the appropriate strategies for each stage.

Overall, the skills for change management require ensuring that the sponsor, those on the performance consultant team, the change targets, and any advocates for the new way of working each fulfill the necessary actions that will decrease resistance and improve the chances that the HPT project will be successful (Connor, 1993; Fuller, 1997).

Teamwork

Because an HPT project is often complex and therefore requires the skills and efforts of more than one person, working in a team is a natural consequence of doing performance consulting. The performance consultant will need to know what actions to take to ensure that the teamwork aspects of the project go smoothly. This means knowing how to set things up and when to intervene to enhance team performance. Delineating roles and responsibilities clearly, providing the necessary communication vehicles, managing meetings, accounting for interdependencies, managing complex scheduling tasks, creating an escalation process for difficulties, and dividing the work into chunks with clear owners and due dates to increase a sense of individual responsibility—these are some of the most important aspects of managing teams.

Working with Experts

Working with experts in related fields can be a challenge. These experts will be used to doing things according to their own models, models that to them seem to be the world's best hope for improving performance. In our experience, experts from other fields often resist working within the HPT framework. Avoiding discussions of which model is better is the first step toward making things go smoothly. Generally there will be some commonality between models. For example, usually there are phases in each performance improvement model that involve figuring out what is going on, determining what to do about it, and then providing some kind of intervention. So at the least you will share a belief in the importance of analysis, design, development, and implementation. Few will argue against measuring results (although many will think it impossible or impractical).

Avoiding conflicts and endless arguments about the efficacy of various models can be accomplished by contracting carefully with experts from other disciplines. The performance consultant will need to define a discrete piece of the analysis or solution creation for the expert to deliver, and also delineate clear expectations for the outcome of that expert's work. If the expert from another field begins to interfere with the integrity of the HPT process, then the performance consultant will need to remind that expert gently to concentrate instead on the piece of the project where that expert can uniquely add value.

Four Major Areas of Specific Expertise

In addition to the general capabilities just reviewed, the performance consultant will need specific expertise in using the human performance system and the HPT model. Using these models requires skills in the following major HPT areas:

1. Conducting analyses
2. Establishing root causes
3. Implementing solutions
4. Evaluating results

Each of these major skill areas will require the application of a number of other skills. Let's examine each area in turn.

Conducting Analyses

The analysis process requires interacting with the customer to deter-mine the business need and what evidence will be accepted at the conclusion of the project to confirm that the business need has been successfully met. This requires the ability to talk with the client about the business in business terms and about HPT in plain lan-guage. It will also be necessary for the performance consultant to consider the system while defining the business issues with the client and to obtain permission from the client to proceed with a performance analysis. The performance consultant will also need to decide, with the client, what measures will be used to determine whether the HPT project has been a success. Validating the success of an HPT project requires a knowledge of the business and of methodologies for collecting metrics to evaluate whether there has been an acceptable return on investment.

Determining the required performance outcomes is tied tightly to the metrics adopted for determining what success will look like. The performance consultant must analyze the business issue and determine what performance would be necessary to solve the prob-lem or to take advantage of the opportunity under consideration. This requires the ability to separate the surface features of perfor-mance from the more important structural features of performance. In other words, the performance consultant must have the ability to determine what results must actually be accomplished to meet business goals, and the ability to avoid being distracted by irrele-vant behaviors that may have been erroneously associated with desired performance in the past (Clark and Estes, 1996; Farrington, 1997). For example, in some situations people become enamored with certain behaviors they associate with necessary performance, for example, the way people dress or what time they arrive at the office. In reality, these behaviors may contribute little or nothing to the business goals these individuals are expected to achieve (Gilbert, 1996).

Also important to analysis is the performance consultant's ability to define the current state and to identify gaps. Interviewing techniques and facilitation may be required for this part of the analysis. Structuring open-ended and closed-ended questions for e-mail surveys, telephone interviews, person-to-person interviews, or focus groups will be required to determine the current state and to identify a first pass at root causes of any barriers to performance. Facilitation skills will be required if focus groups are conducted.

The performance consultant will need to make sure to include in his analysis the relevant parts of the human performance system (using systems thinking). It will also be crucial to pay particular attention to the essential elements of performance gaps and not to be seduced by interesting or highly charged but superficial behaviors that do not have a bearing on the root causes of the performance gaps.

Establishing Root Causes

There are a number of ways to determine the root causes of a performance gap. Using techniques from quality systems, such as fishbone diagrams, affinity diagrams, or interrelationship diagraphs (Brassard, 1996), may prove helpful. Asking "Why?" until the layers of confounding ideas about root causes have all fallen away can also help. Making sure to test the gaps against the three major types of problems—knowledge and skills, motivation, and environment—may prove useful in pinpointing the root causes. Using the human performance system to test the gaps can isolate the root cause: Is it a gap from the organization, the people themselves, their behavior, consequences for performance, feedback, or other environmental factors?

Once the performance consultant is fairly confident that he has adequately determined the root causes, his validation skills will come into play. Observation is often the most reliable way to validate root causes. The performance consultant will need to be aware of observation techniques, including how not to confound the information recovered by making changes in the environment due to the presence of the observer. In some cases, interviews or other methods can be used to validate the root cause findings.

Recommending and Implementing Solutions

Once the problem has been identified and its root causes determined and validated, then the performance consultant will need to recommend solutions. These solutions should be instrumental in eliminating the barriers to performance. They may dovetail to produce an overall effect. The performance consultant, perhaps in concert with individuals who have additional expertise in designing particular solutions, must match root causes with effective solutions. This will require a fluent knowledge of the human performance system and an ability to match interventions with types of root causes.

The performance consultant will need to answer the question, When something is broken in this part of the human performance system, then which interventions are required? The performance consultant will develop and implement the required solutions alone, influence others to do so, or work with others to create and deliver these solutions. This requires influencing, negotiating, project management, teamwork, and perhaps specific skills in developing and implementing particular solutions.

When a solution involves training, the performance consultant either will have himself or will call on someone else who has instructional design expertise. This includes the ability to create or to manage the creation of instructional materials. The instructional design may involve the creation of classroom training, self-instructional training, and a variety of alternative media and delivery systems. The performance consultant must be firmly inoculated against "technolust," the propensity to specify solutions that use the newest available media or delivery system without taking into account the actual requirements of the solution. Performance consultants should be able to correlate the requirements of the learners with the efficiencies inherent in the various options for media and delivery and make the appropriate recommendations (Clark, 1994).

When solutions involve noninstructional interventions, the performance consultant will either need to design and create those interventions or partner with someone who can.

Noninstructional interventions include writing job descriptions, creating feedback systems, redesigning incentive or pay systems, using process engineering, making culture changes, and using change management and information or knowledge engineering.

Evaluating Results

Once interventions have been implemented, the performance consultant must be able to measure the overall success of the project to determine whether the initial goals have been met and the business issue resolved. Evaluation processes actually start in the analysis phase when the decision is made about what to accept as evidence that the business goals have been met. The performance consultant must be able to identify likely evaluation criteria and the attending metrics to collect so that the goals of the project can be identified and validated.

During the project the performance consultant will want to perform a number of evaluative actions, for example, asking for peer review of various stages of the project to ensure that it is on track, requesting client reviews, and establishing a feedback mechanism from members of the group or groups whose performance is being analyzed and changed. The performance consultant will need to devise ways to collect incremental evaluation data that are useful for improving the results of the project.

Once the project is concluded, the performance consultant will need to review the data related to the metrics initially established for the project. This may involve actively collecting and analyzing the data. Or if the original metrics were established based on data that had already been collected, then the performance consultant will simply need to review the current data and compare them to data associated with the performance as it was measured before the project began. Because the interventions designed to remove the root causes of the business issues may take some time to be effective, the performance consultant will need to determine the appropriate timing for measuring the performance changes.

A Performance Technology Mind-Set

For the manager of performance consultants and for performance consultants themselves, looking at problems with an HPT mind-set becomes a crucial characteristic of the way they approach business issues. For example, when a request for services (perhaps for a training course) is made, the person with the HPT mind-set immediately begins to ask questions related to the system within which the business issue occurs. The HPT mind-set requires the performance consultant to look at issues with a systems view. This means not assuming that the presenting problem is the root cause of the issue. It means asking probing questions to see if one or more areas of the human performance system are clearly not in alignment with the desired performance. With practice of HPT skills and with knowledge of an organization, the performance consultant will sometimes be able to determine fairly quickly which part of the human performance system is most likely out of alignment. Validating that initial quick assessment and moving to suggesting solutions can happen rapidly with some issues once the performance consultant has acquired a certain level of expertise. Care must be taken to ensure that solutions are not jumped to prematurely, but the HPT mind-set can be a valuable tool that can drastically reduce the time required to determine the necessary solutions to business issues. This is an advanced skill for senior performance consultants and their managers.

Creating Development Plans

Performance consultants are not created in a day or two, in a month or two, or by completing a project or two. As you can see, quite a few skills are required for successfully navigating HPT projects. To create development plans for performance consultants, you will need to look at short-term and long-term development planning. For suggestions about what skills and capabilities will be required for which HPT roles, see Exhibit 9.1.

Short-Term Development Plans

Short-term development occurs within a year or two of creating a plan to improve knowledge and skills. To grow as a performance technologist yourself or to plan for the growth of your staff, you will need to determine which parts of performance consulting you will do yourself and which parts you will ask others to do. Asking for help in areas where you lack knowledge, skill, or confidence can increase the speed with which you can implement HPT at your company. Not only can others perform tasks that you or your staff are not ready to assume, but they can also serve as coaches or mentors in their areas of expertise.

An excellent way to create a short-term plan for development is to analyze the major goals you have for each potential performance consultant and then determine what skills he or she will need to develop to meet each goal. For example, let's assume that one of your performance consultants has the following goals for this year:

1. Conduct a performance analysis of the customer service response-time problem, recommend solutions, and manage their implementation.

2. Develop and disseminate a process for the selection of alternative learning technologies at Blue Star Enterprises.

3. Create a self-directed study program for the development of the finance community.

As a result of analyzing the skills the performance consultant will need to meet these goals, you may have generated a list of skills like the following: performance analysis, project management,

Exhibit 9.1. Suggested Skills and Capabilities by Role.

Although by no means an exhaustive list, this table provides some suggested skills and capabilities for the different HPT roles.

Role	Skills and Capabilities
HPT sponsor	Business focus, HPT mind-set, interpersonal communications, presentation skills (requires being in a position of influence)
HPT champion	HPT mind-set, change management, business focus, interpersonal communications, presentation skills (also requires respect from members of targeted organization)
Performance consultant	Consulting skills, and a subset of all general and specific HPT skills; specifically, those required to complete assigned projects. Can be augmented by others with specific skills.
Performance analyst	Systemic and systematic approach, conducting analyses, establishing root causes, recommending solutions, interpersonal skills, business focus, working with experts
Root cause analyst	Root-cause analysis, interpersonal skills, business focus, HPT mind-set
Solution developer	Specific expertise in creating interventions such as feedback systems, information systems, compensation strategies, organizational design, training, and so on.
Solution implementer	Expertise in organizing or delivering specific interventions; for example, delivering information sessions, Web-site development, training coordination, training delivery, and organizational design

(continued)

Exhibit 9.1. *continued*

Role	Skills and Capabilities
Partners	Specific expertise and capabilities that will augment those of other project participants, teamwork
HPT consultant or mentor	Expertise in the entire HPT process, including the general capabilities related to it
Project manager	Project management, HPT mind-set, interpersonal skills
Facilitator	Interpersonal skills, specific expertise in running focus groups
Change adviser	Change management, HPT mind-set

process or model development, alternative technology delivery, instructional design, and self-directed learning. If you are unfamiliar with any of these skills, you will need assistance in breaking them down further to determine which subskills the performance consultant may have or may need to develop.

Once you have determined the major skills required to meet each performance consultant's goals, then you will need to assess the performance consultant's current skills, training, or education related to each major skill. Breaking each major skill into subskills is important because the new performance consultant may know how to do part but not all of a major task related to HPT. When that is the case, you will only need to ensure that the performance consultant learns the subskill that is unknown to him or her.

For example, for the performance analysis skill, the performance consultant may know how to analyze the current state, handle interviews and focus groups, and conduct a gap analysis. However, the same performance consultant may be relatively unfamiliar with the language of business or with consulting skills. The performance consultant should develop skills in the aspect of performance analysis that is new and unknown (in this case, the art of business speak and consulting skills).

For each area, make a list of the enhancements or improvements the performance consultant should make. This may include a list of the subskills that need to be learned or practiced if the performance consultant knows what to do but has no experience doing it. In some cases, no improvement may be called for.

Once there is a list of the subskills that need enhancement or improvement, the manager can meet with the performance consultant and the two can then make a decision about what development activities the latter should pursue to obtain or sharpen the necessary subskills. For example, if the performance consultant needs to develop consulting skills, then reading a book, attending a workshop, or shadowing an experienced consultant would be three alternatives for obtaining the necessary skills. The manager and the performance consultant working together can decide the length and breadth of the interventions the performance consultant needs to obtain the required subskills.

Once specific development activities have been identified, then the manager and the performance consultant can schedule due dates for completing each activity. The schedule can include specific dates, the quarter of the fiscal year, or the semester of an academic year when the activity should occur.

For an example of a completed short-term development plan, see Exhibit 9.2.

Long-Term Development Plans

There is only so much that a performance consultant can learn during the first year or two of working in a new role. For long-term development, you can make plans for developing yourself or your department over the next three to five years.

It is hoped that as a result of the planning you have conducted while determining how to implement HPT in your company, you have created or are ready to create an HPT strategic plan. Your

Exhibit 9.2. An Example of a Short-Term Development Plan.

Knowledge and skills required	Current state	Improvements or enhancements	Development activity	Due dates or status
Performance analysis	Can conduct interviews and focus groups, can conduct a gap analysis	Needs business language and consulting skills	Take introduction-to-business class, shadow expert consultant	Business class fall semester, shadowing during second quarter
Project management	Expert	None required	None required	N/A
Process or model development	Has team experience working on an instructional design model	Needs implementation skills	Read and study chapter on implementation by Diane Dormant	Report on developing implementation plans during first quarter
Alternative technology development	Has participated in media and delivery decisions for instructional design projects	Needs updated knowledge of Web delivery	Attend Web conference	February 22 and 23
Instructional design	Has master's degree, six years of varied experience	Needs to enhance evaluation skills	Work on evaluation task force	Meetings start first quarter
Self-directed learning	Experience with programmed instruction, CBT projects	Needs skills related to screen and graphic design	Work with graphic artist on finance project	Phase 2 of project, scheduled for third quarter

HPT strategic plan should support the long-term business needs and strategy of your company. It should paint a picture of how HPT will help your company to realize its business goals.

As we suggested in Chapter Seven, you will want to conduct a performance analysis on your company's readiness to implement HPT. This should help you to zero in on the major development areas that will be required to meet your HPT goals. Make a list of the capabilities that are required from your department to maximize its effectiveness in conducting HPT projects. List the solutions that will be required to achieve those capabilities. Determine who on your staff can be developed to assume the necessary skills, figure out who can partner with your staff to achieve the required results, and assign development areas to individual performance consultants accordingly.

You can also create a staffing plan designed to select new performance consultants for your department who augment your performance consulting skills. When you hire new performance consultants, either because of attrition or because of increased head count, be sure to select people who will add to the combined skills of your current staff.

Development Opportunities

There are any number of ways to acquire new knowledge and skills. Some of the more obvious include training or graduate programs in HPT. Self-directed reading of books, journals, or Web-based references can also assist with development efforts. Attending conferences or professional organization meetings where other performance improvement professionals share their knowledge and skills can provide some of the latest information and developments in the field of HPT. Learning from more experienced HPT professionals can be an invaluable experience, whether in the medium of formal teaching or of informal coaching or mentoring activities.

Studying on one's own or in a formal program, actively working on performance consulting projects, and obtaining feedback from a more knowledgeable performance consultant can provide a most powerful combination of development opportunities. Whenever possible, it would be desirable to arrange the alignment of the following for each performance consultant:

1. Learning opportunities
2. Related performance consulting projects
3. Coaching from someone more knowledgeable

The combination of these three types of development will greatly speed the growth of your performance consultants and will facilitate the development of their expertise.

Summary

In this chapter we have focused on the skills required by individuals who will be performance consultants. Development of these skills can be accomplished in a variety of ways. Determining which skills to develop in which individuals depends on the plans you have for implementing HPT in your department and the compatibility of skills resident or available in both internal and external resources. Here are some main points from this chapter:

- Without competent performance consultants, all other efforts at establishing HPT will be useless.

- Developing individuals should be done in accordance with their performance goals, current strengths, and any gaps in their performance consulting knowledge.

- Being able to talk intelligently about the specific business your company is in is crucial to establishing credibility. This means that your performance consultants can define the market and the customers your company serves, describe the products and services it brings to the market, and trace the organization and processes your company uses to satisfy its customer's needs.

- The knowledge and skills required of performance consultants are many and varied. It may be necessary to form teams to assemble the variety of skills required for a given HPT project.

In the next chapter we look at the requirements and practice of becoming a manager of HPT. The role of the HPT manager is qualitatively different from that of the training manager. Once your department has made the transition, you should experience different requests, have a different focus, and establish different internal alliances. You will want to establish HPT as a business technology, perhaps one that becomes characteristic of the way managers at your company do business.

10

Becoming the Manager of Performance Technology for Your Organization

As HPT becomes established within the organization, it will need a leader to ensure that the HPT program is moving in the right direction and maintains momentum. This chapter will help give you a picture of what it means to be the manager of HPT and how to use it as a tool for ensuring that HPT is developing in strategically important areas.

This chapter pulls together several change management and HPT implementation themes and recommendations that are important for an HPT manager. In some cases, the manager will need to take personal responsibility for a particular role or activity. In other cases, the manager will delegate responsibility; in these cases, the HPT manager's role is to ensure that the delegated activity is well managed.

The role that the HPT manager plays is quite different from the role of an HPT practitioner. It is also significantly different from the role of a training manager. HPT management is not really about doing HPT, and certainly is not about selling training solutions. The purpose of the HPT manager is to create and lead a group whose job focus is helping the organization to obtain results. To achieve this goal, the HPT manager must take on many roles. The manager must lead the HPT effort, provide expertise on HPT practices, forge relationships within the business, ensure the development of further HPT practices, and be the ever-visible and noisy advocate for the adoption of HPT.

Be the Leader of HPT

Every major change initiative needs a strong leader, or it is doomed to flounder (Greenberg, 1994). If HPT is to be developed as a practice and disseminated throughout the organization, the HPT manager must assume a strong leadership role. An organization can have the best HPT process around but if the initiative lacks direction and strategy, HPT practices may never be put to use.

Create the Vision

A change initiative requires a clear picture of the end state to ensure that all efforts are focused on the same outcome (Conner, 1993). The implementation of HPT within your organization is no different. The HPT practitioners need a clear picture of what their role is, and of what implementing the HPT process looks like. Managers need a clear picture of what to expect from performance consultants and need to know how a performance improvement project differs from a training program.

A great vision is not created overnight. Neither is it static. Create a first-pass vision of what HPT can do in your organization and present it to your HPT practitioners. Invite their inputs, criticisms, and recommendations for improvement or clarification. Revise your vision; work on the vision until it generates answers rather than questions. Now present your vision to a few carefully chosen managers and invite their inputs, criticisms, and recommendations. Fine-tune your vision until it is ready to be shown to the entire organization.

The vision must be consistent with the definition of HPT and with the HPT model you have selected or created. The vision should be short, clear, and concise. Ideally, it should fit on a single piece of paper.

Create the Plan

By now you have got our point about needing to take a deliberate and planned approach to implementing HPT within your organization.

Remember, to be successfully implemented all performance improvement projects require a well-designed project plan, and all must be diligently managed (Fuller, 1997). Think of the implementation of HPT as the first and largest performance improvement project that you will implement. Plan appropriately. If project planning is not one of your strong suits, *Managing Performance Improvement Projects* (Fuller, 1997) provides specific strategies, tools, and methods.

You should begin with a clear project definition. This is where the vision plays a major role. The definition indicates what the project will and won't do, what the desired outcomes are, and how the organization will know when the project is successful. The project plan helps to scope the project and establish the priorities.

Once the project definition is complete, you can create the project schedule. What major tasks are necessary to accomplish your HPT implementation goals? When must they be done? Who will do them? The plan aligns your resources to ensure that the implementation is moving forward as rapidly as possible.

After the plan is completed, don't forget to manage it. To remain viable, the plan must receive regular attention, ensuring that tasks are on schedule. People responsible for milestones must be held accountable for accomplishing their tasks on time, as defined in the plan. Otherwise momentum will be lost. Don't forget to pay attention to risk analysis and contingency planning. Be ready to deal with the bumps in the road.

Act Like an Entrepreneur

Establishing an HPT group is rather like starting up a small business. You are offering a new service to the organization that it can either buy into or refuse. Like the owner of a small business, you need to build customer awareness of your existence, establish the value of your service, encourage customer preference for your product, and deliver service that meets the needs of the customer. Based on the funding model under which you operate, you may even get to charge the customer for the service that you provide.

Now is the time for a reality check: What do you know about establishing and running a small business? If your answer is "Not much," you had better fix the situation, and quickly. Your HPT "business" is at stake. You, like other owners of small businesses, should know a shocking business truth: over half of all new small businesses fail to survive their first year. Don't become a casualty.

In his book *The E Myth Revisited* (1995), Michael Gerber identifies why most small businesses go under. It's not because their owners lack technical knowledge of the business they have chosen to enter. A plumber going into business for himself knows how to plumb. A trainer who starts a consulting business for herself knows how to train. What most new business owners lack is entrepreneurial expertise. An entrepreneur knows how to *run* a business, can deal with the responsibilities of creating a marketing and advertising plan, is adept at selling the service to customers, and knows how to grow the business. As the manager of HPT, *you* must become that entrepreneur.

Develop the Management Team

Remember, most business managers do not have a strong background in performance improvement. Usually neither their formal education nor their on-the-job experience has addressed the issues associated with performance improvement. No one else on the management team is contributing to their understanding of systematic performance improvement. They probably don't know what questions to ask. As the manager of performance technology, it's up to you to train and develop the management team in this area. You may not want this responsibility, but it comes with the job.

Your first objective is to shift the business managers' attention from identifying training needs to raising performance issues. Help them to see that raising performance issues is more managerial and strategic than making training requests. Point out that this shift in attention leaves the mundane analysis process to the tacticians and keeps the managers focused on business needs.

Organization managers would like to do a better job of managing performance improvement, but they are probably unsure about what their role is. Start by giving them a new set of questions to ask. Before implementing any performance improvement solutions, managers should ask:

- What business need are we attempting to achieve, and how will it be measured?

- What process was used to analyze the problem and derive the solution(s)?

- What data exist to support the solutions that were selected?

- How do we *know* that these interventions will solve the performance problem?

In addition to making sure that the right questions are asked, you have begun to shift the role and thinking of management regarding performance improvement and HPT.

Next you will want to encourage the business managers to examine the role and impact of performance improvement within the organization. Again, you can greatly accelerate this process by providing them with the right questions to ask. The business managers should be asking the training/human resource development (HRD)/ HPT managers the following strategic questions regarding human capital within the organization:

- What are you doing to improve the performance/worth of our human capital?

- What measurable impact have you had on the business?

- What is the return on investment of our performance improvement efforts?

- How are your efforts driven from the business strategy?

Here's a strategic survival hint: make sure you have really great answers prepared before you give the questions to the business management team.

Be the Expert in HPT

Every significant movement needs a role model. The Boy Scouts had Robert Baden-Powell. The Girl Scouts had Juliet Lowe. Ask any Scout across the world and he or she can tell you the story of their movement's founder. Baden-Powell and Lowe both exemplified the practices they were promoting. They provided a clear and living picture of the role and the goal. As a result, all Scouts know about "Be prepared" and "Do a good deed every day" and strive to do the same themselves. The HPT movement within your organization needs a role model, too.

Increase Your Knowledge of HPT

To be an effective role model, you must be among the most knowledgeable in the organization on HPT. You should understand the fundamentals and foundations of HPT and be able to speak fluently about them. Role models should lead from out in front. Are you in front of your HPT organization's knowledge and understanding of HPT?

As a quick assessment, have you read the *Handbook of Human Performance Technology* (Stolovitch and Keeps, 1992)? Do you remember the names of the leading practitioners? Could you explain the major message of each chapter in the book? If not, read the *Handbook* again. Have you read *Human Competence* (Gilbert, 1996)? Can you explain "Potential for Improved Performance"? Can you discuss the "Cult of Behavior"? If not, create a development plan that puts you out ahead of the organization and keeps you there. Make sure the plan receives adequate attention and effort.

Be Involved in HPT Organizations

To stay ahead in the area of HPT, you should be involved with organizations that are focused on the development of HPT methods and tools and that are sponsoring research in HPT. The International Society for Performance Improvement (ISPI) has been working in this area for years. The American Society for Training and Development (ASTD) is now venturing into HPT. Both organizations offer local as well as international meetings and conferences. Attend some of these meetings. It's the only way to keep up with the field. Tell your manager you'll become obsolete if you don't go.

As you become more seasoned in the HPT field, you may want to increase your involvement in ISPI and/or ASTD. By participating in the work of these organizations, you'll be keeping up with the latest innovations in the field.

Be a Leader in Applied Systems Thinking

Senge's book *The Fifth Discipline* was purchased by hundreds of thousands of business and HRD professionals. Based on our observations, we'd speculate that less than half of those buyers actually read the book. We'd also speculate, based on our conversations with business and HRD managers, that fewer than one in ten understood *The Fifth Discipline*. Systems thinking requires some effort to master. Because HPT looks at performance systemically, you need to be a leader in systems thinking.

There are several good books on systems thinking in addition to *The Fifth Discipline*. Find one that suits you and dive in. Look for systems every day. Seek out and identify cause-and-effect relationships. Draw systems doodles when looking at problems. Spend some time with engineers whenever you can and talk about systems thinking, problem analysis, and troubleshooting.

Establish Relationships with HPT Experts

There is an old proverb that states, "If you want to become an expert, be with experts." The theory is that expertise rubs off. When you spend time with experts from other fields, you begin to understand their perspectives better, see things the way they do, and ask questions like they do. Every role model can use a role model of his or her own.

So how does one build relationships with the experts in the HPT field? Our first recommendation is to attend the international conferences on HPT. The experts are there. They will be giving master's presentations and signing books in the bookstore. They will be giving presentations in the largest rooms available. It won't take you long to develop a mental list of who you want to talk with.

Want to know a secret? Most experts will be delighted to spend time talking with you. Most conference attendees mistakenly assume that the experts are too busy and have no time to engage in dialogue with developing performance technologists. In truth, the experts became experts because early on they learned the importance of sharing their knowledge with others and learning from others. During Jim's first ISPI conference, he found himself in the lunch line behind Tom Gilbert, one of the pathfinders in HPT. As Jim tells the story, "I thanked Tom for writing a valuable book. He asked me to sit with him at lunch. The hour we spent together that day changed my understanding and view of HPT forever."

You should start to develop a file of people and experts you know in the field. Your objective is to establish a relationship with an expert and a practitioner in each of the following HPT disciplines:

- Performance analysis

- Instructional design and technology

- Educational/learning psychology

- Alternative delivery technology

- Mentoring and coaching

- Change management

- Project management

- Reengineering processes

- Quality

- Information technology

- Ergonomics and human factors

- Organization communication

- Compensation

- Feedback systems

Bring HPT and the Business Together

One of the issues associated with the transition from training to performance is HPT's relationship to the business. HPT's purpose is to help the business obtain results. Performance technology is business technology. As the manager of HPT, it's your responsibility to nurture and build the relationship between the business managers and the HPT group. Achieving that goal requires some capabilities that may be new and foreign to you.

Know the Business

An HRD manager was talking to a business manager about his desire to be involved in the strategic planning process. The HRD manager pointed out that he was, after all, responsible for the people component of the business. The business manager asked the HRD manager to describe the company's current business plan. The HRD manager was at a loss, and the discussion immediately ended.

The lesson of this little story is clear. If you want to deal with business issues, you had better understand the business. How well do you understand the business of your organization? Get out a sheet of paper and take this little quiz. We mean it: go get a piece of paper and a pen and then sit down and actually take our test. It's important.

First task: In three or four sentences, describe the business that your organization is in. Your description should be concise, yet comprehensive and compelling. It should flow out of your pen like you are writing your signature.

Next, answer the following questions:

1. What are our three top-selling products or services?
2. What are our three most profitable products or services?
3. What are our three newest products or services?
4. Are revenues for the past quarter up or down compared with last year? By how much?
5. Are orders for the past quarter up or down compared with last year? By how much?
6. Who are our top three competitors?
7. Have you read the annual reports for the last three years? What were the major messages and trends?

Look back on your answers. How did you do? You should have been able to write complete answers to all these questions with coinfidence. If you couldn't do so, you had better create a development plan that gets you up to speed on the business, and fast. You can't sell performance technology as a business technology if you don't know the business.

If you are short on ideas on how to develop in this area, here are a few thoughts to get you started. Get copies of the annual reports and read them. If you need help understanding some of the finer points, seek it out. Attend some trade shows associated with your company's business or products. Schedule short informational interviews with leading business managers to get their take on where the company is headed. Visit the marketing department and obtain copies of product brochures and sales collateral. Get and read the organization's press releases.

Know the Language

Business has a language of its own. So does HPT. A business manager probably won't be excited about learning "HPT speak," so you, as the manager of HPT, will need to learn "business speak." This can be accomplished without going back to school to get an MBA. There are several good books that take a "five-minute MBA" approach and provide the fundamentals. Start to develop a business dictionary so you know the meaning of and the differences between such important business terms as *orders, revenue,* COGS, PPE, ROA, A/R, *shareholder equity,* and *supply chain.*

For an ongoing development strategy, consider subscribing to *Book Summaries*. It has been said that inside every thick business book there is a thin article struggling to get out. *Book Summaries* takes the essentials of business books and distills them down to eight-page overviews. You can keep up with recent popular business books in about two hours per month. A subscription to *Book Summaries* is a great investment for learning business language and the latest business issues.

To establish rapport and a mutually beneficial dialogue with business managers, always be ready with a "hot topic" question. These are the topics that are burning in the minds of the business managers and are certain to initiate conversation. They can be used whenever you encounter a member of the management team: in line at the cafeteria, at the coffee station, or waiting for a meeting to start. The fact that you asked the question shows that you have an interest in the business. The manager's answer may help you to understand the business better, and might even lead to an HPT discussion.

In case you need a few hot topic questions to get started, we asked a couple of senior business managers what issues were keeping them up at night. Here's what they had to say:

- Employee growth and geography/skill shifts: Will our employees be ready for the business needs of tomorrow? Will we have capable employees available when we move into new geographical areas and businesses?

- Employee turnover: Is it good or bad? Are we losing employees who have obsolete skills, or are we losing valuable human capital? How should we manage this?

- Inventory and the impact on our return on assets metrics.

- Asset management: How are we going to effectively manage inventory, plant/property/equipment (PPE), and accounts receivable?

- What can we do to manage cost growth compared with revenue growth?

- How can we sustain our CAGR in terms of real growth? 10 percent growth for a $10 billion company is $1 billion!

- There are new markets we want, but lack the capability/capacity to pursue.

- How do we increase our number of "New to the World Products" versus simple line extensions?

- What can we do to shorten the supply chain?

Based on your growing understanding of the business and the challenges that it faces, you can begin to compile your own list of hot topic questions. As you listen to managers' answers to your questions, look for issues where performance improvement projects could have an impact. Then, when you are ready to take on organization-wide HPT projects, you will already have a candidate list to pursue.

Know the Functions

If your organization is like most others, it is organized around functions and not products or services. This means you probably have functional groups called finance, information systems, marketing, sales, product development (R&D), manufacturing, HRD, and so on. Each group probably has its own charter, processes, and perspective on the world. Not only are these functions your potential clients, they probably will come into play as you design and develop performance improvement solutions based on your performance analyses. Want to change the expense reimbursement standards? Finance might have a few things to say about your plans. Want to launch an electronic performance support system? Information systems might have an opinion on installing it on their servers. Want changes in job descriptions or the compensation system? Expect to hear from HRD.

What do you know about the different functions and departments in your organization? What are their charters? What are their major projects? What are their issues? If you need a significant change in a software system, you don't want to be meeting the information systems manager for the first time. It's far better to have an established relationship with him based on a history of dialogue and understanding when you want assistance or participation in a performance improvement project. As the manager of HPT, you are in the business of forging links with all the different parts of the business. They should understand what you do, what you can do for them, and what you might need to ask them to do for you in the future. Relationships are built on trust, and trust comes partly from knowing who someone is, what she does, and what her needs are.

If you are weak in this area, create a development plan for yourself. If you can't gain experience with the other functions in the organization, at least get some cross-functional exposure. Ask to attend staff meetings to get an understanding of what the hot topics are and what other departments and functions are doing. Get copies of their strategic plans and review them. Spend some time in their organizations. For example, if you want to understand sales and marketing, ask if you can ride along on a couple of sales calls with the local sales rep.

Be the Developer of HPT

As HPT becomes an accepted practice and method within your organization, development will become a growing need. More people will need to begin to use the HPT process that you have defined for the organization. People outside the original HPT group will need more support implementing HPT, so the development of support resources will become a growing need, too.

Develop the People

Implementing HPT from your little HPT group is relatively simple. You can easily watch over and monitor the activities and results of the people who report to you. But as HPT catches on in your organization, your life will become more complex. People outside your group will want to start solving performance problems using your HPT methods, but they won't know how to proceed. As the manager of HPT you are now in the HPT people development business. People will be looking to you and your organization for professional development resources and solutions. If you don't fulfill this need, they will find somebody from outside the organization to help them. The next thing you know, you'll be involved in a model battle. Be ready instead to fulfill this role.

You can fulfil short-term development needs by creating a recommended reading list. What are the books that you would want every new performance technologist to read? If you work for a large global corporation, consider getting into the book distribution business. Finding a copy of the *Handbook of Human Performance Technology* in Jakarta can be very difficult.

You might want to consider offering apprenticeships so that people can be mentored by experienced HPT practitioners. Mentoring provides apprentices with real HPT experience and ensures that they are using the HPT method correctly. It also ensures that they will be working in a manner consistent with your vision for the organization. Depending on your funding model, you can charge the apprentice's manager for teaching his employee, just as if he had been sent off to a workshop.

HPT conferences offer a valuable development opportunity for novice and experienced HPT practitioners alike. Why should the attendance and participation of your organization's members at a conference be random and uncoordinated? Consider leading and coordinating your organization's participation. Organize a company dinner on one night of the conference so that HPT practitioners in your organization can get to know one another. Ask other company participants to indicate their plans for attending various sessions. If you have too many people planning to attend some sessions and few or none planning to attend other sessions, encourage them to spread out and cover the whole conference for the organization. Also encourage people to write up their notes and post them to a single repository where they can be seen and referenced. A central repository will allow people who did not have the opportunity to attend the conference to benefit from what their colleagues learned at the conference.

As your HPT implementation becomes larger, involving more and more people in your organization, consider hosting HPT workshops and conferences within the organization. These workshops and conferences will provide you with a platform for developing the HPT community in a direction consistent with your HPT vision for the organization. If you have a large number of attendees, you can attract important external speakers and workshop leaders to work with your organization. This is a significantly valuable activity that the manager of HPT is positioned to lead.

Develop the Practice

The practice of HPT will be developed over time. New approaches are needed to address increasingly larger and more complex performance improvement projects. New tools can be developed to speed the performance analysis process. You will also want to increase the documentation of your prescribed approach to implementing HPT. This will increase consistency across the organization. It will also allow HPT practitioners to make recommended changes and improvements in a controlled manner.

Be the Advocate for HPT

In order for a performance improvement project to be successful, it needs at least one strong advocate (Conner, 1993; Fuller, 1998). The transition from training to performance improvement is itself a major performance improvement project within your organization. The HPT advocate is responsible for ensuring that HPT remains visible and on the minds of the key managers of the organization. The advocate ensures that success stories are well publicized so that HPT's impact on the organization is well understood. Basically, you want to become the HPT marketing representative and overall cheerleader.

Become a Visible Spokesperson

If you want to sell a new product or service, it needs a strong marketing or awareness program. Telling the potential customer or client about the service just once is inadequate. They need to be continually reminded of the service, and how it will help them be successful. Talk to somebody in your advertising or marketing department if you need to be convinced of this fact.

As the HPT manager for your organization, you own the responsibility for the HPT awareness and marketing strategy. What are your plans for continually expanding, improving, and clarifying the awareness and understanding of HPT throughout your organization? Mentioning it once is not enough.

You will need to develop a really great presentation on HPT. Think of your presentation not only as informative but also as an extended commercial for the product. Practice the presentation until you can do it perfectly. Get help with your presentation if you need assistance or coaching. Once you and the presentation are ready, go on the road. Solicit invitations to large group staff meetings to provide an update on the latest in performance improvement. Talk to groups of individual contributors, too. When any group is willing to listen to your message, be there for them. Remember to include lots of examples in your presentation, and practice making the case examples real.

Become an HPT Storyteller

Everybody loves a great story. They are engaging, and we enjoy hearing the exploits of others and how the story ends. Stories are an effective teaching and communication tool because stories are memorable. People remember stories almost ten times more frequently than facts alone (Egan, 1989). You may not recall much that was written in Chapter Two, but if you are like most folks, you'll remember the story of Bubber. When we worked for the Hewlett-Packard Company, we discovered that the organization's culture and values were communicated through the telling of "Bill & Dave stories" (Bill Hewlett and Dave Packard). By sharing stories about the activities and decisions of the company's founders, Hewlett-Packard managers and employees passed on the company's culture to others.

Every successful HPT project is a story. It begins with a need that is unmet in the organization. There are people and personalities involved. There is a process and a series of events. Finally, there is a conclusion with results. Telling an HPT story will keep people interested, but more important, it will enable them to visualize what the implementation of HPT looks like. Storytelling is a very important tool for the HPT advocate. Learn to do it well, and begin to amass your collection of stories to share with others when the opportunity presents itself. Practice now. Can you tell the Bubber story?

Publish Results

Whenever the organization completes a performance improvement project, make certain that you capture the results. Even if it was not your group that implemented the HPT project, get the results. Nothing speaks like results. Keep track of the cumulative contribution of HPT to the organization over time. Track dollars saved, sales increased, quantity improved, and timeliness achieved. Do not allow the HPT contribution to go unpublished and unrecognized.

The results should be included in a presentation that you give to everyone in the organization. You should also create case study write-ups that show the results obtained. Don't be afraid to make internal press announcements heralding the latest accomplishments of the group or the organization.

Summary

In this chapter we have pulled together many of the themes and recommendations that we made throughout the book. We wanted to create a vivid picture of the responsibilities associated with becoming an HPT manager. The manager of HPT has several roles that need to be fulfilled in order for the organization to be successful with the transition from training to performance.

The role of the leader must be fulfilled if the transition is to have direction and maintain momentum. Developing HPT practitioners need a visible expert who can serve as a role model for their newly chosen profession. Somebody must bring the business and HPT together, building understanding and forging relationships. HPT will continue developing and somebody needs to lead the development of the next generation of tools and practices. Finally, the HPT group needs an advocate who can communicate the role and value of HPT to the organization.

We hope you'll be that person, and we wish you the best of luck.

References

Aronson, E. *The Social Animal.* (7th ed.) New York: Freeman, 1995.

Beckwith, H. *Selling the Invisible: A Field Guide to Modern Marketing.* New York: Warner Books, 1997.

Bellman, G. M. *The Consultant's Calling: Bringing Who You Are to What You Do.* San Francisco: Jossey-Bass, 1992.

Block, P. *Flawless Consulting: A Guide to Getting Your Expertise Used.* San Francisco: Pfeiffer, 1981.

Brassard, M. *The Memory Jogger Plus+.* Methuen, Mass.: GOAL/QPC, 1996.

Champy, J. *Reengineering Management.* New York: HarperCollins, 1995.

Clark, R. E. "Media Will Never Influence Learning." *Educational Technology Research and Development,* 1994, *42*(3), 21–29.

Clark, R. E. "Motivating Performance: Part 1—Diagnosing and Solving Motivation Problems," *Performance Improvement,* 1998, *37*(8), 39–47.

Clark, R. E., and Estes, F. "Cognitive Task Analysis." *International Journal of Educational Research,* 1996, *25,* 403–417.

Conner, D. *Managing at the Speed of Change.* New York: Villard Books, 1993.

Dormant, D. "Implementing Human Performance Technology in Organizations." In H. D. Stolovitch and E. J. Keeps (eds.), *Handbook of Human Performance Technology: A Comprehensive Guide for Analyzing and Solving Performance Problems in Organizations.* San Francisco: Jossey-Bass, 1992.

Egan, K. *Teaching as Story Telling.* Chicago: University of Chicago Press, 1989.

Ely, D. P., and Minor, B. B. *Education Media and Technology Yearbook.* Englewood, Colo.: Libraries Unlimited, 1994.

Farrington, J. R. "The Impact of Structural Features and Context on Improving Transfer in Concept Acquisition." Unpublished doctoral dissertation, University of Southern California, Los Angeles, 1997.

Fuller, J. L. *Managing Performance Improvement Projects*. San Francisco: Jossey-Bass, 1997.

Fuller, J. L. "Making the Transition to a Focus on Performance." In J. Robinson and D. G. Robinson (eds.), *Moving from Training to Performance: A Practical Guide*. San Francisco: Berrett-Koehler, 1998.

Galpin, T. J. *The Human Side of Change: A Practical Guide to Organization Redesign*. San Francisco: Jossey-Bass, 1996.

Gerber, M. E. *The E Myth Revisited*. New York: HarperCollins, 1995.

Gilbert, T. F. *Human Competence: Engineering Worthy Performance*. (Tribute ed.) Washington, D.C.: International Society for Performance Improvement, 1996.

Greenberg, J. (ed.). *Organizational Behavior: The State of the Science*. Hillsdale, N.J.: Erlbaum, 1994.

Harless, J. H. *An Ounce of Analysis (Is Worth a Pound of Objectives)*. Newnan, Ga.: Harless Performance Guild, 1975.

Hertzberg, F. "One More Time: How Do You Motivate Employees?" *Harvard Business Review*, Jan.–Feb. 1968, pp. 35–42.

Kirkpatrick, D. L. *Evaluating Training Programs*. Madison, Wisc.: American Society for Training and Development, 1975.

Kleiner, A. *The Age of Heretics: Heroes, Outlaws, and the Forerunners of Corporate Change*. New York: Doubleday, 1996.

Mager, R. F. *What Every Manager Should Know About Training*. Atlanta, Ga.: Center for Effective Performance, 1992.

Mager, R. F. *Goal Analysis* (3d ed.). Carefree, Ariz.: Center for Effective Performance, 1997.

Martin, J. *The Great Transition: Using the Seven Disciplines of Enterprise Engineering to Align People, Technology, and Strategy*. New York: AMACOM, 1995.

Micklethwait, J., and Wooldridge, A. *The Witch Doctors: Making Sense of the Management Gurus*. New York: Times Books, 1996.

Pascale, R. T. *Managing on the Edge*. New York: Touchstone Books, 1991.

Pfeffer, J. *Competitive Advantage Through People*. Boston: Harvard Business School Press, 1994.

Pritchett, P. *The Quantum Leap Strategy*. Dallas, Tex.: Pritchett & Associates, 1991.

Ries, A., and Trout, J. *Marketing Warfare*. New York: McGraw-Hill, 1986.

Robbins, S. P. *Essentials of Organizational Behavior*. (5th ed.) Englewood Cliffs, N.J.: Prentice Hall, 1997.

Rummler, G. A., and Brache, A. P. "Transforming Organizations Through Human Performance Technology." In H. D. Stolovitch and E. J. Keeps (eds.), *Handbook of Human Performance Technology: A Comprehensive Guide for Analyzing and Solving Performance Problems in Organizations.* San Francisco: Jossey-Bass, 1992.

Rummler, G. A., and Brache, A. P. *Improving Performance: How to Manage the White Space on the Organization Chart.* (2d ed.) San Francisco: Jossey-Bass, 1995.

Senge, P. M. *The Fifth Discipline: The Art and Practice of the Learning Organization.* New York: Doubleday, 1990.

Southwest Airlines. "Southwest Airlines 1997 Annual Report." Located on-line at [http://www.iflyswa.com/financials/investor_relations.html]. 1998a.

Southwest Airlines. "Southwest Airlines Fact Sheet." Located on-line at [http://www.iflyswa.com/press/factsheet.htm]. 1998b.

Stolovitch, H. D. "Calculating the Return on Investment in Training: A Critical Analysis and a Case Study." Paper presented at the 1998 annual meeting of the International Society for Performance Improvement, Chicago, Mar. 1998.

Stolovitch, H. D., and Keeps, E. J. *The Handbook of Human Performance Technology.* San Francisco: Jossey-Bass, 1992.

Stolovitch, H. D., Keeps, E. J., and Rodrigue, D. "Skill Sets for the Human Performance Technologist." *Performance Improvement Quarterly*, 1995, 8(2), 40–67.

Tufte, E. R. *Envisioning Information.* Cheshire, Conn.: Graphics Press, 1990.

About the Authors

Jim Fuller is the principal consultant for Redwood Mountain Consulting (RMC). He is responsible for assisting client organizations with the strategic implementation of performance consulting, mentoring new performance consultants, and conducting workshops to develop performance improvement professionals.

Before joining RMC, Jim was director of learning and performance technology at the Hewlett-Packard Company (HP), where he worked for eighteen years. His organization represented HP's R&D efforts in the area of learning and performance, with specific responsibility for performance improvement processes, instructional design methods, education evaluation systems, and the application of technology to accelerate learning. Jim created HP's performance consulting group, led the development of performance technology practices, and developed HP's performance improvement consultants.

Jim has held management positions in R&D, manufacturing, marketing, engineering, sales, support, and education. He holds an M.S. degree in instructional and performance technology from Boise State University and is currently pursuing an Ed.D. in performance technology at the University of Southern California.

He has authored the book *Managing Performance Improvement Projects* and is a contributing author to *Work Based Education, Moving from Training to Performance: A Practical Guide,* and to the second edition of the *Handbook of Human Performance Technology.* He is a frequent speaker at conferences held by the International Society for Performance Improvement, where he was an advocate representative, and the American Society for Training and Development. He has spoken on implementing performance technology, evaluation strategies, use of technology in training delivery, metacognition in learning, and gender-based communications in the workplace. He has also been an invited guest lecturer at several universities.

Jeanne Farrington is president of Redwood Mountain Consulting. She is responsible for conducting performance improvement analyses, developing customized strategic plans for performance improvement initiatives, and providing assistance of various kinds to people who want to improve the way learning and performance are supported in their organizations.

Jeanne has more than fifteen years of experience in the field of performance technology. She has developed hundreds of training courses and performance improvement projects, either as manager, lead designer, team member, or consultant. Before she founded RMC, Jeanne worked at Sun Microsystems, Silicon Graphics, and Hewlett-Packard. During that time she was responsible for management and executive programs, manufacturing training, and employee and educator development.

Jeanne has an M.A. degree in instructional technology from San Jose State and an Ed.D. degree in educational psychology and technology from the University of Southern California (USC). She is an adjunct professor at USC, where she assisted with the design of their graduate programs in human performance at work.

Jeanne is a frequent speaker at the International Society for Performance Improvement and the American Society for Training and Development. She is also a member of the American Educational Research Association and the American Psychological Association.

The authors may be contacted via e-mail at the following addresses:

jim@redwoodmtn.com
jeanne@redwoodmtn.com
http://www.redwoodmtn.com

International Society for Performance Improvement

The International Society for Performance Improvement (ISPI) is the leading international association dedicated to improving productivity and performance in the workplace. Founded in 1962, ISPI represents more than ten thousand members throughout the United States, Canada, and in nearly forty other countries. Monthly meetings of over sixty different chapters provide professional development, services, and information exchange.

ISPI's vision is to be the preferred source of information, education, and advocacy for improving workplace performance through the application of Human Performance Technology (HPT)—a process of selection, analysis, design, development, implementation, and evaluation of programs to most cost-effectively influence human behavior and accomplishment. The Society's mission is to improve the performance of organizations in systematic and reproducible ways through the application of HPT. Assembling an annual conference and other educational events, producing several periodicals, and publishing dozens of books and resources, including the *Handbook for Human Performance Technology*, are some of the ways ISPI works toward achieving this mission.

ISPI members include performance technologists, training directors, human resource managers, instructional designers, human factors practitioners, and organizational development consultants. ISPI members work in more than three thousand organizations, including Fortune 500 companies, governmental agencies, the military, academic institutions, consulting businesses, and other organizations.

ISPI makes a difference to people by helping them grow into skilled professionals who use integrated and systematic approaches to add value to their organizations and to the profession. Whether designing training programs, building selection or incentive systems, assisting organizations in their own redesign, or performing myriad other interventions, ISPI members produce results.

ISPI makes a difference to organizations by increasing professional competence and confidence. ISPI members help organizations anticipate opportunities and challenges and develop powerful solutions that contribute to productivity and satisfaction.

ISPI makes a difference to the field of performance technology by expanding the boundaries of what the industry knows about defining, teaching, supporting, and maintaining skilled human performance. By supporting research and development, providing information on a variety of technologies, and facilitating membership interaction, ISPI members use approaches and systems that ensure improved productivity.

For additional information, please contact

International Society for Performance Improvement
1300 L Street, N.W., Suite 1250
Washington, D.C. 20005
Telephone: (202) 408-7969
Fax: (202) 408-7972
Website: www.ispi.org
E-mail: info@ispi.org

Index